Featuring over 150 recipes from the James Beard Foundation Award–winning chef and author of *Root to Leaf*, *Vegetable Revelations* offers innovative, adaptable, and delicious ways to serve a wide range of vegetables.

At Miller Union, his hugely successful Atlanta restaurant, Steven Satterfield is constantly searching for new ways to serve the vast variety of foods offered each season. When it comes to cooking meat and seafood, there are specific guidelines for doneness—but each vegetable has inherent properties that can be enhanced or manipulated in infinite ways, offering numerous opportunities to innovate.

In *Vegetable Revelations*, Satterfield explores how texture affects the eating experience, how globally inspired ingredients can make vegetables more compelling, and how valuing every part of a plant is the key to creative cooking. Best of all, he provides flavor-packed recipes that celebrate the delicious diversity available to us, arranged by botanical families and culinary categories, including Roots, Leaves, Stalks, Brassicas (broccoli, brussels sprouts, cauliflower), Legumes, Nightshades (eggplant, tomatoes, bell peppers, potatoes), Cucurbits (cucumbers, zucchini, watermelon, squash), and Mushrooms.

The recipes offered here cover breakfast, lunch, dinner, desserts, beverages, and snacks. There's also a section on textural toppings, flavor-forward sauces, spice blends, and condiments that can be mixed and matched to enhance any simply prepared vegetable. While vegetarians and vegans will love these recipes, there are some fabulous dishes that include meat, poultry, and seafood as well.

Illustrated with sumptuous photographs throughout, *Vegetable Revelations* will broaden your kitchen know-how, open new doors for exploration and adventure, and give you fresh and flavorful ideas for great meals that omnivores, vegetarians, and vegans alike will adore.

VEGETABLE REVELATIONS

Also by Steven Satterfield

ROOT TO LEAF

VEGETABLE
REVELATIONS

INSPIRATION FOR
PRODUCE-FORWARD COOKING

Steven Satterfield
with Andrea Slonecker

PHOTOGRAPHY BY ANDREW THOMAS LEE

HarperCollins books may be purchased for educational,
business, or sales promotional use. For information,
please email the Special Markets Department at
SPsales@harpercollins.com.

FIRST EDITION

Design by Elina Cohen

Library of Congress Cataloging-in-Publication Data

Names: Satterfield, Steven, author. | Lee, Andrew Thomas,
photographer.

Title: Vegetable revelations : inspiration for produce-
forward cooking / Steven Satterfield with Andrea Slonecker;
photography by Andrew Thomas Lee.

Identifiers: LCCN 2022041763 (print) | LCCN 2022041764
(ebook) | ISBN 9780063088030 | ISBN 9780063088047 (epub)

Subjects: LCSH: Cooking (Vegetables) | LCGFT: Cookbooks.

Classification: LCC TX801 .S29 2023 (print) | LCC TX801
(ebook) | DDC 641.6/5–dc23/eng/20220906

LC record available at https://lccn.loc.gov/2022041763

LC ebook record available at https://lccn.loc.gov/2022041764

ISBN 978-0-06-308803-0

23 24 25 26 27 TC 10 9 8 7 6 5 4 3 2 1

This book is dedicated in loving memory of my former assistant and motherly protector Rebecca Harrigan, who stood by my side for many years as my greatest cheerleader and dear friend. Every time we had a photo shoot for this book, we lit a candle in her honor and felt her presence guiding us along.

CONTENTS

RECIPES BY CHAPTER

FOREWORD

When I set out to write this book, I had a basic premise: take a vegetable, and decide how to prepare it right now to show off its best attributes. This may sound similar to my first work, *Root to Leaf*, but time has elapsed, and my style has naturally evolved. I am now cooking through a different lens and outside of my normal repertoire. I have found new inspiration, living in a multicultural city with access to a global pantry, and from my travels abroad, tasting different flavors and considering all the possibilities. These kinds of experiences have changed how I think about food, and they filter through my mind to emerge as the recipes that are now printed in the pages that follow.

But the process of making this book became very different. By the time we moved into production, we were at the beginning of the COVID-19 pandemic. There were a lot of things in motion that had to come to a complete halt. Suddenly time stopped and everything changed. Before the pandemic struck, I could often take a little time off here and there from running a busy restaurant to work on a collection of recipes or photograph dishes. In this crisis, however, I had to tend to the mothership, Miller Union, first. Without our beloved, well-established restaurant, I would not even be writing a book. Between navigating waves of COVID surges and employee absences, pivoting to take-out meals or outdoor dining, and meetings with the Independent Restaurant Coalition to lobby Congress for financial relief, I found very little free time to develop recipes or even schedule shoots.

This book became somewhat of an experiment. But amid all the turmoil, I had assembled a trusty, masked-up cookbook team to help keep the project moving along. There were times when I had to figure out a dish on set in front of the camera (in photographer Andrew Thomas Lee's backyard studio), which was sometimes exciting and sometimes frustrating, but it allowed for free-flowing creativity without a scripted recipe. I remember the prop stylist, Thom Driver, often asking me what a dish was going to look like and I would sometimes say, "We are all about to find out for the very first time." There were some failures, and some reshoots, but most were triumphs and delights.

I always started with great ingredients, and I followed my instincts to the end. My methodical culinary assistant, Alex Lampert, watched my hands and took detailed notes as I guided us through a process or technique. Coauthor Andrea Slonecker, who lives 2,600 miles and three time zones away in Portland, Oregon, collaborated virtually and tested every single recipe for the entire project. We were never once in the same room until the final days of finishing the manuscript, when we sequestered ourselves in a remote and beautiful lakeside setting to complete our work.

One silver lining to the pandemic is that home cooking has had a major resurgence, and these recipes reflect that curiosity and the spirit of trying something new or different that you may have not made space for in the past. The influences that shaped these recipes are genuine and authentic, and have opened my eyes to new ways of cooking; in particular, cooking vegetables. There is still so much to learn about the food of other cultures, and I want to emphasize that I am no expert on any one cuisine, except perhaps the foodways of the South, where I was raised. I have a curious mind and an open heart, and I've witnessed that food can teach us immeasurable lessons. Good food can bridge gaps, unite differences, and make peace if we tune our minds and taste buds to it. My mantra: Eat more vegetables, try new things, and never stop learning.

INTRODUCTION

Culinary revelations come to me in many forms. When I travel and try different cuisines. When I'm collaborating with chef friends and taste their dishes. Or even when I'm just reading recipes. There's often a vegetable technique or a notion that draws me in.

Traveling in Oaxaca, I probably tasted over twenty versions of mole. Some were made by street vendors, and others were served in fancy restaurants, but most were in the form of a sauce for meats. I immediately thought, *How would this flavor profile taste when applied to vegetables?* I took inspiration from these mole flavors and fused them with my own style of cooking by using ground dried chiles, cacao nibs, and pumpkin seeds to make a crunchy topping to coat earthy-sweet roasted parsnips.

In London I tasted an Indian saag that was so delicious I found myself craving it when I returned home. Though I didn't know the exact recipe, I could recall the taste of the sweet, warming spices and the punch of ginger. It reminded me of a dish of braised greens with handfuls of fresh coconut that a friend from Kerala once made me. One day in my kitchen, I decided to marry these two taste memories on the fly, using what was readily available to sauté: some spinach and mustard greens with garam masala, ginger, and coconut flakes.

At a little restaurant in Siena, Italy, I was served a savory kale crostini with creamy chicken liver mousse and a sour cherry conserva. My mind was blown by the fascinating emerald-green toasts. In broken Italian, I quizzed the chef about what I was eating. From what I could understand, the bread was dipped in a liquid mixture of whisked egg and pureed *cavolo nero*, or lacinato kale. Now I borrow this idea to make use of stale bread, slicing it thick and griddling it for a greens-soaked savory French toast.

As a chef who's been a proponent of plant-focused cooking for years, I'm more inspired by cooking with plants than with proteins. I find the dynamic nature of their availability intriguing as they come in and out of season. Vegetables are my muse, and the star of my meals, while animal proteins take a supporting role. Though these recipes center around vegetables, this is a cookbook for omnivores and vegetarians alike. I believe we all need to eat meat more responsibly and less frequently, and a big part of that shift is putting more plants on our plates.

I grew up in the South, and my food has always reflected that, but my style is still evolving. Since writing my first book, *Root to Leaf*, I've started to venture out of my comfort zone, applying new-to-me flavor profiles and techniques that I wouldn't have before. Lately, I've turned to other cultures for vegetable inspiration, and it's reinvigorated my joy of cooking. I want you to take my lead on this and dive in, venturing outside of your comfort zone too.

As you cook through this book, remember: When produce is at its peak, it simply tastes best. All you need to do is find the vegetables that inspire you, at a farm stand or your local store, and buy what looks fresh and good. Take that inspiration to prepare these produce-forward recipes, or make up your own twists. The goal is to get you excited about cooking in your kitchen and experience your own vegetable revelation.

MY COOKING STYLE

Technique and Texture

When presented with a particular vegetable, I contemplate all of its possibilities. Will it be gently blanched just to bring out some subtle sweetness? Can it be charred and smoky, or broiled and caramelized? Will it be slow-simmered or flash-fried? Whichever cooking technique I choose to use, I consider the desired outcome first and then apply a bit of reverse engineering to get there. Knife work plays a key role in determining the texture of a dish. How a vegetable is cut—diced or minced, chopped or torn, shaved or grated—changes how it feels in the mouth, and how the flavors mingle on your palate.

Flavor

I consider the inherent flavor of a vegetable first and how to bring out its best attributes, then how to complement those flavors with other ingredients that lift them up. Think of roasting beets with vinegar to both bring out their fruity side and contrast their earthiness. Or adding spices and herbal sauces to any simply prepared vegetable to wake up its flavor.

Serving Temperature

The temperature of a dish when it is served is critical to the eating experience. Some things are best served piping hot, like a comforting soup or stew, or ice-cold, like a refreshing cocktail or wedge of watermelon. But there is also a middle ground where many dishes taste best. A cool yogurt sauce will temper a blistered vegetable hot off the grill, and the contrasting temperatures and textures evolve as you take each bite. Flavors are more perceptible to the palate when a food is eaten in that middle ground—and you'll see that some of my dishes are served warm-ish or room temperature.

Cooking

I use all edible parts of vegetables, from the roots to the leaves and everything in between. Those leaves at the top of celery stalks can be used like herbs, while beet greens make a hearty salad. Where one person may see vegetable scraps, I see opportunities. Fall squash seeds are delicious roasted, and asparagus bottoms make a silky soup. Carrot tops can be used as the bulk of a flavorful herby sauce. If there is a way to use it, I'm going to find it and I encourage you to, also.

WHAT I'VE LEARNED FROM COOKING WITH STEVEN

A note from coauthor Andrea Slonecker

I'm the one who meticulously scrapes every last streak of batter out of a bowl with a rubber spatula and chops that final little bit of onion near the root. I've always saved my leek tops to make stock with the spent chicken bones from last night's dinner, because I just hate wasting food.

What I've learned from Steven has taken my own no-waste practice a step further. There are parts of vegetables that I never considered worth saving, but now do: things like fennel stalks, broccoli stems, and squash seeds. His recipes have taught me that fennel stalks can be used interchangeably with the bulb, perhaps sliced thinly for a crunchy salad. I now peel the bottoms of broccoli stems and cut them into tender coins for roasting, and puree squash seeds to thicken soup.

Although it happened mostly virtually, and during a global pandemic, Steven and I have spent three years cooking together to write this book. In this time my own style has evolved by following his charmingly frugal cooking philosophy—with benefits to both my wallet and the planet—and yours will too.

HOW TO USE THIS BOOK

We divided this book into two parts for ease of use. First, you'll find a diverse list of odds and ends to consider as building blocks. They are a collection of staple recipes to mix and match with vegetables. They are used as accents in the main recipes later in the book, but you can apply these spice blends, savory sauces, crunchy toppings, and more to enhance any vegetable preparation. Keep them in your back pocket for creating flavor, texture, and nuance in your cooking.

Part II features the main vegetable recipes. In these chapters, each vegetable is grouped by type, or by its botanical family, and you'll find a wide variety of cooking techniques to explore their possibilities. These recipes cover the bases, from breakfast, lunch, and dinner, through desserts, beverages, and snacks. We've made these recipes produce-focused, approachable, and adaptable. Feel free to take liberties to account for what's on hand and have fun with it.

You'll notice that most recipes suggest that you taste and adjust the seasoning. That goes beyond adding just a pinch of salt. Does it need more brightness in the form of lemon or vinegar? Are the spices coming through? What about mouthfeel—does it need another drizzle of olive oil or slather of sauce? These are all questions to ask yourself as you taste. Take the liberty to adjust the ingredients to be sure there is a nice balance between salty, sweet, bitter, and tart on your palate.

PART I

Building Blocks

FLAVOR AND TEXTURE ENHANCERS
FOR VEGETABLES

SPICE BLENDS

Spices come from all over the globe and add dimension and bold flavor, transforming a simple vegetable dish into an extraordinary one. Many spices cross cultural lines, and certain combinations evoke the taste of specific regions of the world. Use these blends to transport your cooking. Grinding whole spices in a spice grinder or a mortar and pestle yields a fresher flavor. For a more intense flavor, toast the whole spices in a dry skillet to maximize their potential.

A SIMPLE CURRY POWDER

Makes about ¼ cup

My redux version minimizes the shopping list but not the flavor.

1 tablespoon coriander seeds

1 tablespoon cumin seeds

2 teaspoons fennel seeds

2 teaspoons fenugreek seeds

2 teaspoons yellow mustard seeds

1 tablespoon ground turmeric

1 teaspoon ground cayenne

Combine the coriander, cumin, fennel, fenugreek, and mustard seeds in a medium skillet and set it over medium heat. Cook, swirling and stirring the seeds around in the pan, until they smell toasted and take on a slightly darker hue, about 2 minutes. Transfer the toasted spices to a plate to cool, then pulverize in a spice grinder or mortar and pestle to a powder. Transfer to an airtight container and mix in the turmeric and cayenne. The spice blend will keep in a dark place at room temperature for up to 6 months.

GARAM MASALA

Makes about ½ cup

A sweet, warming Indian spice blend to use in everything from pumpkin pancakes to creamed greens.

2 tablespoons coriander seeds

2 tablespoons cumin seeds

1 tablespoon green cardamom pods

1 tablespoon whole black peppercorns

1 (3-inch) cinnamon stick

1 teaspoon whole cloves

1 teaspoon freshly grated mace or nutmeg

Combine the coriander, cumin, cardamom, peppercorns, cinnamon stick, and cloves in a medium skillet and set it over medium heat. Cook, swirling and stirring the spices around in the pan, until they smell toasted and take on a slightly darker hue, about 2 minutes. Transfer the toasted spices to a plate to cool, then pulverize in a spice grinder or mortar and pestle to a powder. Transfer to an airtight container and mix in the mace or nutmeg. The spice blend will keep in a dark place at room temperature for up to 6 months.

RAS EL HANOUT

Makes about ¼ cup

A heady, intoxicating Moroccan-inspired blend of sweet and savory spices to flavor slow-cooked stews. While many versions are made with a multitude of spices, this mixture utilizes easier-to-find pantry staples for the home cook.

2 teaspoons cumin seeds

1½ teaspoons coriander seeds

8 green cardamom pods

1 teaspoon fennel seeds

1 teaspoon allspice berries

1 teaspoon black peppercorns

2 teaspoons ground ginger

1 teaspoon ground turmeric

1 teaspoon ground cinnamon

1 teaspoon ground cayenne

½ teaspoon ground clove

Combine the cumin, coriander, cardamom, fennel, allspice, and peppercorns in a medium skillet and set it over medium heat. Cook, swirling and stirring the spices around in the pan, until they smell toasted and take on a slightly darker hue, about 2 minutes. Transfer the toasted spices to a plate to cool, then pulverize in a spice grinder or mortar and pestle to a powder. Transfer to an airtight container and mix in the ginger, turmeric, cinnamon, cayenne, and clove. The spice blend will keep in a dark place at room temperature for up to 6 months.

QUATRE ÉPICES

Makes about ¼ cup

France's original pumpkin spice, with the zing of white pepper.

2 tablespoons freshly ground
white peppercorns

1 tablespoon freshly grated nutmeg

1 tablespoon freshly ground clove

1 tablespoon ground ginger

Combine the pepper, nutmeg, clove, and ginger in an airtight container. The spice blend will keep in a dark place at room temperature for up to 6 months.

AJIKA SEASONING BLEND

Makes about ¼ cup

We can thank the Republic of Georgia for this hot pepper spice blend, the foundation for the country's most prominent condiment of the same name.

2 dried guajillo chiles, stemmed,
seeded, and coarsely chopped

4 green cardamom pods

1 teaspoon fenugreek seeds

1 teaspoon cumin seeds

1 teaspoon dried oregano

1 teaspoon ground sumac

Combine the chiles, cardamom, fenugreek, and cumin in a medium skillet and set it over medium heat. Cook, swirling and stirring the ingredients around in the pan, until they smell toasted and take on a slightly darker hue, about 2 minutes. Transfer the toasted spices and chiles to a plate to cool, then pulverize in a spice grinder or mortar and pestle to a powder. Transfer to an airtight container and mix in the oregano and sumac. The spice blend will keep in a dark place at room temperature for up to 6 months.

ZA'ATAR

Makes about ½ cup

Dried herbs and seeds combine in this crunchy blend for topping vegetables, hummus, and other Middle Eastern delights.

2 tablespoons sesame seeds

1 tablespoon cumin seeds

1 tablespoon coriander seeds

2 tablespoons dried marjoram or oregano

1 tablespoon ground sumac

1 tablespoon dried thyme

½ teaspoon medium-grain sea salt

Combine the sesame, cumin, and coriander seeds in a medium skillet and set it over medium heat. Cook, swirling and stirring the ingredients around in the pan, until they smell toasted and take on a slightly darker hue, about 2 minutes. Transfer the toasted seeds to a plate to cool, then pulverize in a spice grinder or mortar and pestle to a powder. Transfer to an airtight container and mix in the marjoram or oregano, sumac, thyme, and salt. The spice blend will keep in a dark place at room temperature for up to 6 months.

STOCKS AND BROTH

Whenever you're prepping vegetables, consider your castoffs. Things like leek tops, fennel fronds and stalks, and parsley stems can be thrown into a stockpot instead of the compost bin. This notion will influence the flavor of the stock as you cook seasonally throughout the year. In the fall, use mushroom stems for umami and squash seeds to add sweetness. In the winter, root vegetable scraps and brassica stalks bring earthy tones. Come spring, think green and utilize spent pea pods, green garlic, and tender herb stems. Summertime calls for corncobs, green bean tips, and overripe tomatoes, which all add body and depth to your seasonal stock. For chicken stock, utilize the remains of your roast chicken dinner and add the bones to the pot. A richly flavored mushroom broth made with dried porcini is wonderful in risotto, soups, and sauces—keep this one simple, and do use the rehydrated mushrooms in your cooking.

SEASONAL VEGETABLE STOCK

Makes about 4 quarts

1 pound coarsely chopped onions, such as leek tops, unpeeled sweet onions, shallots, or a mix

6 ounces celery or fennel stalks and butts

6 ounces carrots, parsnips, or other sweet vegetables or scraps

1 head garlic, halved, or 1 bunch coarsely chopped green garlic

1 small handful thyme sprigs, parsley stems, or other herbs (not mint)

1 bay leaf

1 teaspoon whole black peppercorns

Any seasonal vegetable scraps on hand (optional)

Put everything in a stockpot and cover by 1 inch of water. Place the pot over medium-high heat and bring to a simmer. Decrease the heat to maintain a gentle simmer and cook for 1 hour.

Strain the stock through a fine-mesh sieve into a heatproof container and discard the solids. The stock will keep in an airtight container in the refrigerator for up to 1 week, or in the freezer for up to 6 months.

PORCINI MUSHROOM BROTH

Makes about 3 cups

1 ounce dried porcini mushrooms

1 small sweet onion, coarsely chopped

3 cloves garlic

3 sprigs fresh thyme

Mushroom stems and scraps (optional)

Combine the dried mushrooms, onions, garlic, thyme, and mushroom scraps if you have them in a 4-quart saucepan and cover with 8 cups of water. Place over medium-high heat and bring to a simmer. Decrease the heat to maintain a gentle simmer and cook for 40 minutes. Strain the liquid through a fine-mesh sieve into a heatproof container, reserving the solids for another use, such as in the Maximo Mushroom Risotto (page 286), pasta, or soup. The broth will keep in an airtight container in the refrigerator for up to 1 week, or in the freezer for up to 6 months.

ROASTED CHICKEN STOCK

Makes about 4 quarts

1½ to 2 pounds roasted chicken bones, or the leftover carcass from a whole roasted chicken

12 ounces coarsely chopped onions, such as leek tops, unpeeled sweet onions, shallots, or a mix

4 ounces celery or fennel stalks and butts

4 ounces carrots, parsnips, or other sweet vegetables or scraps

1 head garlic, halved, or 1 bunch coarsely chopped green garlic

1 small handful thyme sprigs, parsley stems, or other herbs (not mint)

1 bay leaf

1 teaspoon whole black peppercorns

Any seasonal vegetable scraps on hand (optional)

Put everything in a stockpot and cover by 1 inch of water. Place the pot over medium-high heat and bring to a simmer. Decrease the heat to maintain a gentle simmer and cook for 1 hour.

Strain the stock through a fine-mesh sieve into a heatproof container and discard the solids. The stock will keep in an airtight container in the refrigerator for up to 1 week, or in the freezer for up to 6 months.

CREAMY CONDIMENTS

Cool and creamy things add contrasting mouthfeel and flavor to vegetable dishes. My go-tos are almost always mayo- or yogurt-based condiments for spreading, slathering, and dipping. While working on these recipes, we experimented with seemingly every possible way of forming an egg-oil-acid emulsion in what we called our "mayo lab." Our preferred method for small-batch mayo and aioli is a quart jar and an immersion blender. The trick is to carefully trickle in the oil at first until the emulsion forms. If you don't have an immersion blender, you can use a regular blender or food processor, but you'll need to double the batch to have enough volume for those larger gadgets. Follow the instructions carefully, as emulsions can easily break if you add the oil too quickly. Yogurt sauces are easy—just start with thick Greek yogurt and whisk in flavors that will enhance the dish.

HOMEMADE MAYONNAISE

Makes 1 heaping cup

2 egg yolks

2 teaspoons fresh lemon juice

2 teaspoons apple cider vinegar

1½ teaspoons kosher salt

1 teaspoon mustard powder

1 cup canola oil

In a wide-mouth, quart-size glass canning jar, combine the egg yolks, lemon juice, vinegar, salt, and mustard powder. Blitz with an immersion blender until the mixture is foamy. Now set the jar on a kitchen towel to keep it stable. With the blender running at the bottom of the jar, slowly trickle in the oil until it begins to thicken and becomes velvety smooth, indicating an emulsion has formed. At this point you can drizzle in the oil in a steadier stream while moving the blender wand up and down until the oil is all incorporated. Add a splash of water if it becomes too thick. The mayonnaise will keep in an airtight container in the refrigerator for up to 5 days.

VARIATION: CHIPOTLE MAYO

Stir in 1 grated garlic clove, 1 teaspoon finely grated lime zest, 1 teaspoon chipotle powder, and 1 teaspoon smoked paprika to the finished mayonnaise.

VARIATION: MALT VINEGAR MAYO

Substitute 2 tablespoons of malt vinegar for the lemon juice and apple cider vinegar.

LEMONY AIOLI

Makes 1 heaping cup

1 whole egg

2 tablespoons fresh lemon juice, plus 1 teaspoon finely grated lemon zest

2 cloves garlic, grated

1 teaspoon fine sea salt

1 cup extra virgin olive oil

In a wide-mouth, quart-size glass canning jar, combine the whole egg, lemon juice and zest, garlic, and salt. Blitz with an immersion blender until the mixture is foamy. Now set the jar on a kitchen towel to keep it stable. With the blender running at the bottom of the jar, slowly trickle in the oil until it begins to thicken and becomes velvety smooth, indicating an emulsion has formed. At this point you can drizzle in the oil in a steadier stream while moving the blender wand up and down until the oil is all incorporated. Add a splash of water if it becomes too thick. The aioli will keep in an airtight container in the refrigerator for up to 5 days.

VARIATION: SAFFRON AIOLI

Substitute ½ teaspoon saffron threads for the lemon zest.

HONEYED LEMON YOGURT

Makes 1 heaping cup

1 cup plain Greek yogurt

2 tablespoons extra virgin olive oil

2 teaspoons fresh lemon juice, plus
1 teaspoon finely grated lemon zest

1 teaspoon honey

½ teaspoon kosher salt

In a small bowl, whisk together the yogurt with the oil, lemon juice and zest, honey, and salt. Taste for seasoning and adjust to your liking. The yogurt will keep in an airtight container in the refrigerator for up to 3 days.

CURRIED YOGURT

Makes 1 heaping cup

1 cup Greek yogurt

1 tablespoon plus 1 teaspoon
A Simple Curry Powder (page 4),
or store-bought is fine

1 tablespoon fresh lemon juice,
plus 1 teaspoon finely grated
lemon zest

1 clove garlic, grated or pressed

1 teaspoon kosher salt

In a small bowl, whisk together the yogurt, curry powder, lemon juice and zest, garlic, and salt. Taste for seasoning and adjust to your liking. The yogurt will keep in an airtight container in the refrigerator for up to 3 days.

VINAIGRETTES

Vinaigrettes are all about balance. The acidic component lifts a dish and adds brightness, while the fat counterpoints with rich mouthfeel. Together they are a conduit for flavor and that's where you can have fun with it. Make variations with mustards, alliums, herbs, spices, honey, or even bolder ingredients like miso, anchovies, or hot chiles. For delicate leafy salads, I dress the sides of the salad bowl and gently toss the leaves to lightly coat them, or sometimes I just drizzle the dressing across the top of the finished salad to keep the leaves from wilting. Hardy greens, vegetables, and grains can be more aggressively dressed to match their robust flavors and textures.

FRENCH VINAIGRETTE

Makes about 3/4 cup

1/4 cup red wine vinegar

1 tablespoon fresh lemon juice, plus 1/2 teaspoon finely grated lemon zest

1 clove garlic, grated or pressed

1 teaspoon Dijon mustard

1 teaspoon kosher salt

1/2 teaspoon freshly ground black pepper

6 tablespoons extra virgin olive oil

In a small bowl, whisk together the vinegar, lemon juice and zest, garlic, mustard, salt, and pepper. Drizzle in the olive oil while whisking to emulsify. Taste for seasoning. The vinaigrette will keep in an airtight container in the refrigerator for up to 5 days.

CORIANDER VINAIGRETTE

Makes about 2/3 cup

2 teaspoons coriander seeds

1/4 cup white wine vinegar

2 teaspoons whole-grain mustard

1 teaspoon kosher salt

1/2 teaspoon freshly ground black pepper

6 tablespoons extra virgin olive oil

Place the coriander seeds in a small skillet over medium heat and toast until they smell aromatic and take on a slightly darker hue. Cool completely, and then grind to a coarse powder in a spice grinder or a mortar and pestle.

In a small bowl, whisk together the vinegar, mustard, salt, pepper, and ground coriander. Drizzle in the olive oil while whisking to emulsify. Taste for seasoning. The vinaigrette will keep in an airtight container in the refrigerator for up to 5 days.

CHILE VINAIGRETTE

Makes about ²/₃ cup

2 tablespoons white balsamic vinegar

Juice and zest of 1 lime

1 teaspoon fine sea salt

¼ cup extra virgin olive oil

1 teaspoon chopped fresh oregano leaves

1 serrano chile, minced

In a small bowl, whisk together the vinegar, lime juice and zest, and salt. Drizzle in the olive oil while whisking to emulsify. Add the oregano and chile. Taste for seasoning. The vinaigrette will keep in an airtight container in the refrigerator for up to 5 days.

SUMAC VINAIGRETTE

Makes about ³/₄ cup

3 tablespoons white wine vinegar

1 tablespoon honey

1 tablespoon fresh lime juice, plus ½ teaspoon lime zest

1 clove garlic, grated or pressed

1 teaspoon ground coriander

1 teaspoon ground sumac

1 teaspoons kosher salt

½ cup extra virgin olive oil

In a small bowl, whisk together the vinegar, honey, lime juice and zest, garlic, coriander, sumac, and salt. Drizzle in the olive oil while whisking to emulsify. Taste for seasoning. The vinaigrette will keep in an airtight container in the refrigerator for up to 5 days.

BAGNA CAUDA VINAIGRETTE

Makes about ¾ cup

1 (2-ounce) tin anchovies

3 tablespoons sherry vinegar

1 clove garlic, minced

1 teaspoon Dijon mustard

1 teaspoon honey

½ teaspoon kosher salt

½ cup extra virgin olive oil

1 tablespoon chopped fresh parsley

1 tablespoon chopped fresh mint

Drain the anchovies and place them in a small bowl. Using the tines of a fork, mash the anchovy filets to break them into small bits. Mix in the vinegar, garlic, mustard, honey, and salt. Drizzle in the olive oil while whisking to emulsify. Add the parsley and mint. Taste for seasoning. The vinaigrette will keep in an airtight container in the refrigerator for up to 1 day.

MISO VINAIGRETTE

Makes about ¾ cup

¼ cup white miso paste

2 tablespoons fresh lemon juice

2 tablespoons unseasoned rice vinegar

1 clove garlic, grated or minced

⅓ cup canola oil

4 green onions, thinly sliced

In a medium bowl, whisk together the miso, lemon juice, vinegar, and garlic until relatively smooth. Drizzle in the canola oil while whisking to emulsify. Add the green onions. Taste for seasoning. The vinaigrette will keep in an airtight container in the refrigerator for up to 5 days.

CRUNCHY TOPPINGS

Technically the word "crunch" means to make a loud sound when chewing, by crushing a firm ingredient between your teeth. But it is so much more! Crisp textures can enliven the eating experience, particularly when eaten in concert with tender vegetables, silky soups, or simple salads. Here are a few of my favorite crunch factors that are used throughout the recipes in this book.

ROASTED NUTS OR SEEDS

Makes as much as you'd like

Roasting nuts and seeds brings out a richer, deeper flavor and crunchier texture. Always set a timer because they go from perfectly toasted to burnt rather quickly.

As many whole, chopped, sliced, or slivered nuts or seeds as you'd like to toast (usually 1 to 2 cups)

Heat the oven to 350ºF. Spread the nuts or seeds on a rimmed baking sheet and roast until they smell and look nicely toasted, shaking them around the pan once or twice as they roast. Well-roasted nuts will have a deep, nutty brown color when one is broken open; seeds will have a golden brown exterior. Most whole nuts take 8 to 12 minutes. Seeds, smaller nuts, and chopped, sliced, or slivered ones will go more quickly, so check them after just a few minutes in the oven. Keep in mind they will continue to crisp as they cool after roasting.

Transfer the roasted nuts or seeds to a plate and set aside to cool completely. They will keep in an airtight container at room temperature for up to 2 weeks.

TOASTED COCONUT (FLAKED OR DESICCATED)

Follow the instructions for roasted nuts, stirring after 3 minutes in the oven. Toast until the coconut is lightly browned, checking often, 5 to 6 minutes total.

GARLIC CROUTONS

Makes about 3 cups

A good crouton has plenty of fat, is well seasoned, and is crunchy on the outside with a subtle give in the middle. For uniformity, cut the bread into cubes, or tear it by hand for a more rustic version that's even crunchier. The finished croutons can be ground into bread crumbs for a textural topping.

½ loaf stale pain au levain, sourdough, or any country-style bread, cut or torn into 1-inch pieces (about 3 cups)

¼ cup extra virgin olive oil

2 cloves garlic, minced

1 teaspoon kosher salt

Heat the oven to 350ºF. In a large bowl, toss the bread cubes with the oil, garlic, and salt until the bread is evenly coated and soaks up the oil. Turn the cubes out onto a rimmed baking sheet and bake until the croutons are crisp but not brittle (they will continue to crisp out of the oven), 10 to 12 minutes. Set aside to cool completely. The croutons will keep in an airtight container at room temperature for up to 5 days.

TOASTED GARLIC BREAD CRUMBS

To make bread crumbs, pulse the cooled croutons in a food processor until they are as coarse or as fine as you'd like.

CRISPY CURED HAM

Makes as much as you'd like

The salt-cured, air-dried hams of Spain, Italy, and the American South can be transformed into a crispy, crumbly topping for salads, soups, and hors d'oeuvres. Use serrano, prosciutto, or country ham to make this elevated version of bacon bits.

Extra virgin olive oil

Thinly sliced serrano, prosciutto, or country ham

Heat a slick of oil in a wide nonstick skillet over medium heat. Lay 2 to 3 slices of ham in the pan with as little overlap as possible and cook until it's wrinkled and the fat is golden brown, about 2 minutes per side. As the first batch of slices begin to shrink in the pan, you can add more. Remove the slices as they are done. You'll know they are crisp when they stop bubbling because the moisture within the meat has been cooked out. Set the ham on a plate to cool and continue to crisp, then break the slices up into pieces. They will keep at room temperature for up to one day.

CRUNCHY FRIED FIELD PEAS OR BEANS

Makes about 1½ cups

Use cooked chickpeas, black-eyed peas, or any similarly sized legume to make a great snack for eating out of hand, or serve them as a crunchy accoutrement. They take a starring role in the Spicy Cocktail Mix on page 199.

1½ cups cooked shelled beans or peas (homecooked, frozen, or canned), drained and rinsed

About 1¼ cups canola oil for frying

Fine sea salt

Place the cooked beans or peas in a clean kitchen towel and roll them around until dry. Pour enough oil into a 10-inch skillet so that it's about ½ inch deep. Place the skillet over medium heat until the oil reaches 350°F on an instant read thermometer. Line a tray with paper towels and set it near the stove.

When the oil is to temperature, fry the legumes until golden and crispy, 6 to 8 minutes, adjusting the heat as needed. Use a slotted spoon to transfer the fried legumes to the tray, and season them with salt while they are still hot. Serve warm or at room temperature. After cooling to room temperature, the fried legumes will keep in an airtight container for up to 1 week.

CRISPY FRIED SHALLOTS AND SHALLOT OIL

Makes about 1 cup

A flavor powerhouse in South Asian cooking, this method for slowly frying shallots makes them brittle-crisp with a sweet umami flavor. The frying oil becomes infused with the shallot flavor too and can be used for stir-frying and in dressings and marinades.

2 large shallots, peeled

1 cup peanut or vegetable oil

Fine sea salt

Using a mandoline or sharp chef's knife, slice the shallots into ⅛-inch-thick rounds. Separate the slices into individual rings. Set a small mesh sieve over a bowl for the shallots to drain when they are done frying, and line a plate with paper towels to cool them on.

Combine the shallot rings and oil in a small saucepan and place it over high heat. Cook until the rings wilt down enough to be completely submerged in the oil, 1 to 2 minutes. Decrease the heat to medium and gently fry the shallots, stirring often, until they are golden brown, 15 to 18 minutes. (They will continue to darken and crisp out of the oil, so be careful not to overcook.)

Immediately strain the fried shallots through the sieve, collecting the infused oil in the bowl. Spread the shallots on a paper-towel-lined plate and sprinkle with sea salt. Set aside to cool and crisp. After cooling to room temperature, the fried shallots will keep in an airtight container for up to 1 week. The shallot oil will keep in an airtight container in the refrigerator for up to 1 month.

MOLE CRUNCH

Makes about ½ cup

Mole is a rich sauce from the state of Oaxaca, Mexico, with a deep complexity. I concocted a spice blend inspired by these flavors with coarsely ground cinnamon, cacao nibs, pumpkin seeds, and currants that is vibrant and exciting on anything it touches.

2 tablespoons roasted pumpkin seeds (see page 24)

2 tablespoons raisins or currants, coarsely chopped

2 tablespoons cacao nibs

1 tablespoon toasted sesame seeds

1 tablespoon toasted cumin seeds

1 small cinnamon stick, broken up

1 guajillo chile, stemmed, seeded, and coarsely chopped

Place all of the ingredients in a food processor and pulverize until everything is broken up into a uniform, coarse, crumbly mixture. The mole crunch will keep in an airtight container at room temperature for up to 1 week.

EVERYTHING SEASONING

Makes about ¼ cup

This popular bagel topping is a tasty, crunchy accent for more than just boiled bread. It's particularly nice with whipped chèvre on whole radishes (see page 71) as a fun party starter.

1 tablespoon dried onion flakes

1 tablespoon dried garlic flakes

1 tablespoon black or toasted sesame seeds, or a combination

1 tablespoon poppy seeds

1 teaspoon fennel seeds or caraway seeds, coarsely crushed

1 teaspoon flaky sea salt

Combine all ingredients in an airtight container and shake to mix. The seasoning will keep in a dark place at room temperature for up to 6 months.

FLAVOR BOMBS

Here's some ammunition to make your vegetable dishes explode with flavor. Elements of umami, citrus, chiles, spices, and flavorful fats work their way into these palate-pushing condiments. Keep these in your back pocket when you want to accent a dish and make a big impression.

GARLIC CONFIT AND GARLIC OIL

Makes about ¾ cup

Garlic confit is simply garlic submerged and cooked in fat, resulting in soft, spreadable cloves and really flavorful oil. I prefer this to roasting a head of garlic, as it has a better yield, it's less messy, and I just like the subtle flavor. This will work in any recipe in place of roasted garlic, and the fragrant garlic-infused oil is great for dipping bread and delicious in salad dressings. Note that you can make this on the stove or in the oven.

1 head garlic, cloves separated and peeled

About 6 tablespoons extra virgin olive oil

For the stovetop, place the garlic cloves in a butter-warming pot and add enough oil so they are just completely covered. Set the pot over medium-low heat and cook until the garlic is bubbling and golden brown, 10 to 12 minutes. Remove from the heat and set aside to cool, leaving the garlic in the oil.

For cooking in the oven, preheat the oven to 350°F. Place the garlic cloves in an 8-ounce ramekin and add enough oil so they are just completely covered. Set the ramekin on a small baking sheet (this makes handling much easier) and roast for 20 minutes. Turn the oven off and let it rest in the oven for 5 minutes to gently finish cooking. Remove from the oven and set aside to cool, leaving the garlic in the oil.

For either method, note that if you cook the garlic too long, it can burn or become tough, so be sure to keep an eye on it as it starts to turn color. Once cooled, transfer the garlic confit and oil into an airtight container and store in the refrigerator for up to 2 weeks.

LIME-PICKLED RED ONIONS

Makes about 1½ cups

Use this quick method for pretty pink pickled onions to add color and brightness to tacos, burgers, salads, and really anything that would benefit from a little crunch and gripping acidity.

1 small red onion, trimmed and peeled

Juice of 2 large limes (about ⅓ cup)

1 teaspoon fine sea salt

Using a mandoline or sharp chef's knife, slice the onion as thinly as possible into rings. Toss the onions with the lime juice and salt in a small bowl, separating the rings. Macerate until the onions are softened and bright pink in color, stirring occasionally, about 1 hour. The pickled onions will keep in an airtight container in the refrigerator for up to 1 week.

PONZU

Makes about ⅓ cup

Ponzu is a delightful combination of soy sauce with yuzu juice and can some-times have fish flakes or seaweed in it for umami. It is traditionally used as a glaze for tataki or as a dipping sauce for sashimi, but I love it as a layer of fla-vor for vegetables like asparagus, turnips, or cucumbers. I use lime and orange juices when I don't have access to yuzu.

1½ tablespoons mirin

1 tablespoon unseasoned rice vinegar

1 tablespoon soy sauce

1 tablespoon fresh lime juice

1 tablespoon fresh orange juice

In a small bowl, combine the mirin, vinegar, soy sauce, lime juice, and orange juice and set the ponzu aside. The ponzu will keep in an airtight container in the refrigerator for up to 1 week.

QUICK COCONUT-CILANTRO CHUTNEY

Makes about 2 cups

This chutney makes a great dip for crunchy fried potatoes and can be a condi-ment for any Indian-inspired vegetable preparation.

1 (14-ounce) can coconut milk

1 bunch cilantro (including stems), washed and chopped

1 serrano chile, stemmed and chopped

½ cup unsweetened shredded coconut

3 tablespoons fresh lime juice

2 teaspoons kosher salt

1 teaspoon minced fresh ginger

Combine the coconut milk, cilantro, chile, shredded coconut, lime juice, salt, and ginger in a food processor and blitz until mostly smooth but still somewhat tex-tured. The chutney will keep in an airtight container in the refrigerator for up to 3 days.

GREEN CHILE SAMBAL

Makes about 1 cup

Indonesian in origin, sambal is a spicy-tart condiment that I like to keep around in the fridge. The genesis for my version came from a bumper crop of hot green chiles, and I was looking for ways to use them. The addition of tamarind makes this a somewhat sweet rendition.

2 dried guajillo chiles, stemmed and torn in half

1 stalk lemongrass

2 shallots, roughly chopped

2 jalapeño chiles, coarsely chopped

2 serrano chiles, coarsely chopped

1 (1-inch) piece fresh ginger, peeled and coarsely chopped

1 (1-inch) piece fresh turmeric, peeled and coarsely chopped

2 cloves garlic, peeled and halved

¼ cup vegetable oil

2 tablespoons tamarind paste (see Note on page 274)

1 tablespoon light brown sugar

1 tablespoon fish sauce

Place the guajillo chiles in a small bowl and cover with boiling water. Let soak for 10 minutes, then drain. Trim and discard the hard root end and top two-thirds of the lemongrass, leaving the bottom 3 inches. Peel away the tough outer layers to reveal the tender, innermost stalk and coarsely chop it. Place the rehydrated guajillo chiles, lemongrass, shallots, jalapeño, serrano, ginger, turmeric, and garlic in a food processor and blitz to a uniform, chunky paste, about 2 minutes.

Place a medium skillet over medium-low heat and add the oil. Carefully spoon the chile mixture into the warm oil. Increase the heat to medium and cook, stirring constantly until the smell is fragrant and the mixture is sizzling, 2 to 3 minutes. The goal here is to emulsify the oil with the chiles and cook out some of the water through evaporation. Add the tamarind paste, brown sugar, and fish sauce and cook until combined, about 1 minute. Remove the pan from the heat and let the sambal cool to room temperature. The sambal will keep in an airtight container in the refrigerator for up to 2 months.

SWEET PEPPER HARISSA

Makes 1½ cups

I use fresh sweet peppers to balance the heat of smoky dried chiles in this take on the addictive North African chile sauce.

2 smoky dried chiles,
such as chipotle, ancho,
or morita

2 tablespoons extra virgin olive oil

1 pound sweet red peppers,
such as red bell, pimiento, or
sweet Italian varieties, diced

2 shallots, diced

2 cloves garlic

1½ teaspoons kosher salt

1 teaspoon ground caraway

1 teaspoon ground coriander

1 teaspoon ground cumin

1 tablespoon tomato paste

1 tablespoon fresh lemon juice

Place the dried chiles in a small bowl and cover with boiling water. Let soak for 10 minutes, then drain and set aside. Heat the oil in a medium saucepan over medium heat. Add the sweet peppers, shallots, garlic, and salt and cook, stirring frequently, until they are beginning to soften, about 5 minutes. Add the rehydrated chiles, caraway, coriander, and cumin and continue to cook and stir until the shallots are translucent and the peppers are softened, about 5 minutes. Add the tomato paste and lemon juice and cook, stirring constantly, until the tomato paste begins to caramelize on the bottom. Remove the pan from the heat and transfer the contents to a blender. Blend until very smooth, scraping down the sides as needed. Taste for seasoning and adjust as needed. The harissa will keep in an airtight container in the refrigerator for up to 1 week.

SPICED TOMATO JAM

Makes about 2 ¾ cup

One of my go-tos for roma tomatoes is this aromatic savory-sweet jam. Serve it alongside cheese, or better yet, in a grilled cheese sandwich. It's also the base for the Cherry Tomato Crostata on page 214.

¼ cup extra virgin olive oil

4 shallots, coarsely chopped

2 tablespoons minced ginger

1 tablespoon minced garlic

2 tablespoons kosher salt

2 ½ pounds roma tomatoes, chopped (about 6 cups)

1 tablespoon fresh thyme leaves

1 teaspoon ground cumin

½ teaspoon freshly ground black pepper

⅛ teaspoon ground mace

⅛ teaspoon ground clove

½ cup apple cider vinegar

⅓ cup packed dark brown sugar

In a Dutch oven over medium heat, warm the oil. Add the shallots, ginger, garlic, and salt and sweat for 5 minutes, stirring frequently. Add the chopped tomatoes, thyme, cumin, pepper, mace, and clove. Continue to cook over medium heat, stirring often, until the tomatoes break down and the mixture comes to a simmer, about 5 minutes. Add the vinegar and brown sugar and stir well. Continue to cook until the mixture has thickened to a jam-like consistency, 40 to 50 minutes. Be sure to stir frequently to avoid sticking and scorching, and decrease the heat as needed when it begins to spatter as it gets close to being done. It will continue to thicken a bit as it cools, so remove it from the heat when it is still a little looser than a jam consistency. Let cool to room temperature. The jam will keep in an airtight container in the refrigerator for up to 2 weeks.

SEAWEED-CHILE BUTTER

Makes about ¾ cup

A novel idea for a compound butter is to use dried seaweed and chiles for the complex flavor and a dark moody color. I like to melt it over warm roasted root vegetables, especially sweet potatoes (see page 56).

½ cup wakame or nori (see Note)

1 dried guajillo chile, stemmed, seeded, and coarsely chopped

1 dried ancho chile, stemmed, seeded, and coarsely chopped

½ cup (1 stick) unsalted butter, at room temperature

Juice and zest of 1 lime, at room temperature

2 teaspoons kosher salt

1 clove garlic, grated or pressed

Combine the wakame and dried chiles in a blender and pulverize to a powder. In a medium bowl, combine the wakame and chiles with the softened butter, lime juice and zest, salt, and garlic. Using a fork, mash the ingredients until they come together, and then stir with the tines of the fork until well incorporated. The butter can either be wrapped in parchment and rolled into a log for slicing or pressed into a ramekin or small bowl to serve with a knife. It will keep wrapped tightly in the refrigerator for up to 2 weeks or frozen for up to 2 months. Bring to room temperature before using.

NOTE: Wakame and nori are both types of edible seaweed sold dried in many grocery stores and natural-food markets. Wakame is typically packaged as small, dehydrated ribbons, while nori is most often sold as sheets for making sushi. If using nori, coarsely crumble the sheets before measuring.

MAÎTRE D' BUTTER

Makes about 1¼ cups

The first step to making this classic compound butter is to cook the shallots in red wine and vinegar to infuse the flavor into the alliums. The result is a gorgeous, savory butter with ruby-red flecks of shallots and emerald-green herbs.

1 small shallot, finely diced

¼ cup dry red wine

1 tablespoon red wine vinegar

1 teaspoon kosher salt

½ cup (1 stick) unsalted butter, at room temperature

1 tablespoon chopped fresh parsley

1 tablespoon chopped fennel fronds or fresh tarragon

1 tablespoon finely sliced fresh chives

1 clove garlic, minced

1 teaspoon finely grated lemon zest

Combine the shallots, wine, vinegar, and ½ teaspoon of the salt in a small skillet and cook over medium-low heat until all the liquid completely evaporates, 5 to 7 minutes. As it evaporates, stir the shallots to make sure no liquid is clinging to them in the bottom of the pan. Remove the pan from the heat just as the last bit of moisture is gone but before the shallots begin to scorch. Scrape the shallots onto a small plate to cool.

In a medium bowl, combine the butter, cooled shallots, parsley, fennel fronds or tarragon, chives, garlic, lemon zest, and remaining ½ teaspoon of salt. Using a fork, mash the ingredients until they come together, and then stir with the tines of the fork until well incorporated. The butter can either be wrapped in parchment and rolled into a log for slicing or pressed into a ramekin or small bowl to serve with a knife. It will keep wrapped tightly in the refrigerator for up to 2 weeks or frozen for up to 2 months. Bring to room temperature before using.

SAVORY SAUCES

Here is a collection of some of my favorite finishing sauces, from classic French techniques to variations on pesto, romesco, salsa, and more. Sauces are the ultimate way to add pizzazz to your plate. Mix and match these with simple vegetable preparations throughout the book and keep some around for adding impromptu final touches.

BEURRE BLANC OR BEURRE ROUGE

Makes about 1 cup

A modernized, slightly less rich version of a classic butter sauce. Use white wine for more delicately prepared vegetables, and red when they are grilled or caramelized.

1½ cups dry white or red wine (white for blanc, red for rouge)

1 teaspoon white wine vinegar or red wine vinegar (white for blanc, red for rouge)

1 shallot, chopped

1 clove garlic, chopped

1 sprig thyme

1 bay leaf

10 black peppercorns

½ teaspoon kosher salt

½ teaspoon granulated sugar

6 tablespoons cold butter, sliced, plus more as needed

In a small saucepan, combine the wine, vinegar, shallots, garlic, thyme, bay leaf, peppercorns, salt, and sugar. Set the pan over medium-high heat and bring to a simmer. Cook at a gentle simmer until the liquid is reduced to 3 tablespoons, 15 to 20 minutes. Strain the mixture over a bowl and discard the solids. Measure the yield of the reduction; if it is more than 3 tablespoons, return the liquid to the pan and continue reducing; if it is less, add water back.

Return 3 tablespoons of the reduced wine back to the pan and place it over low heat. Using a small whisk or a fork, add one slice of cold butter at a time, whisking constantly. The goal is to keep the liquid moving as the butter melts, so it emulsifies. As one cube is almost melted, add the next. Once the last bit of butter goes in, turn the heat off and keep whisking until emulsified and glossy. If you want the sauce to be thicker or richer, you can add another tablespoon or two of butter, but I like the balance of flavors at this ratio.

LIME TAHINI SAUCE

Makes about ⅓ cup

Lime gives a simple twist to this creamy Middle Eastern sauce for fried, roasted, or grilled vegetables.

¼ cup tahini

1 tablespoon fresh lime juice, plus ½ teaspoon finely grated lime zest

1 clove garlic, grated or pressed

1 teaspoon kosher salt

Whisk the tahini, lime juice and zest, garlic, and salt in a small bowl and add just enough water to give it a spreadable, saucy consistency. The sauce will keep in an airtight container in the refrigerator for up to 3 days. Bring to room temperature before serving.

SALSA VERDE

Makes about 1 cup

Not to be confused with the tomatillo- and cilantro-based Mexican salsa, this Italian version is my go-to sauce when I have a plethora of herbs on hand. It's a catch-all for nearly any in the crisper drawer. Spoon it over roasted or grilled vegetables, meats, or fish.

1 cup mixed finely chopped herbs, such as parsley, cilantro, mint, tarragon, fennel fronds, celery leaf, or carrot tops

2 tablespoons capers, chopped

1 tablespoon fresh lemon juice, plus 1 teaspoon finely grated lemon zest

1/2 to 2/3 cup olive oil

Kosher salt, to taste

In a medium bowl, mix the herbs, capers, and lemon juice and zest. Drizzle in enough oil to make it saucy. Taste for seasoning and add salt, if needed. This sauce is best served at room temperature on the day it is made.

CHIMICHURRI

Makes about 1 cup

A variation on salsa verde is this Argentine green sauce with a touch of heat from dried chiles and flavored with cumin. Though it is traditionally served with grilled beef, I love it even more with vegetables.

1/2 cup finely chopped cilantro leaves and stems

1/4 cup finely chopped flat-leaf parsley leaves and stems

2 tablespoons finely chopped fresh oregano leaves

1 small shallot, minced

2 cloves garlic, minced

1 teaspoon crushed red pepper

1 teaspoon freshly ground cumin

1 teaspoon kosher salt

1/2 teaspoon freshly ground black pepper

1/2 cup extra virgin olive oil

1 tablespoon red wine vinegar

In a medium bowl, mix the cilantro, parsley, oregano, shallots, garlic, red pepper, cumin, salt, and pepper. Add the oil and vinegar and whisk until well combined. Taste for seasoning and adjust to your liking. This sauce is best served at room temperature on the day it is made.

CARROT TOP CHERMOULA

Makes about 1½ cups

When you buy fresh carrots with tops, save them to make this zesty North African herb sauce, and pair it with the grilled carrots on page 53. If you happen to have preserved lemon on hand, use it instead of lemon zest and skip the salt.

1 packed cup carrot top leaves

green onions, finely chopped

½ cup fresh flat-leaf parsley, finely chopped

½ cup fresh cilantro, finely chopped

1 clove garlic, finely chopped

1 teaspoon cumin seeds, coarsely ground

1 teaspoon coriander seeds, coarsely ground

1 teaspoon sweet paprika

1 teaspoon fine sea salt

1 tablespoon fresh lemon juice, plus 1 teaspoon freshly grated lemon zest

¾ cup extra virgin olive oil

Fill a medium bowl with water and add the carrot leaves. Swish the leaves in the water, then transfer them to a salad spinner basket to drain and spin dry (or drain them in a colander and wrap them in a paper towel). Finely chop the carrot top leaves and place them in a medium bowl. Add the green onions, parsley, cilantro, garlic, cumin, coriander, paprika, salt, and lemon juice and zest. Drizzle in the olive oil and whisk with a fork. This sauce is best served at room temperature on the day it is made.

SPRING HAZELNUT–HERB PESTO

Makes about 2 cups

We normally think of pesto as that magical Genovese combination of basil, garlic, pine nuts, and Parmigiano-Reggiano in a suspension of really good olive oil. In this rendition, I use delicate spring herbs and swap out the nuts and cheese for a delicious new flavor profile.

1 cup mixed sweet herbs, such as parsley, chervil, dill, fennel fronds, and tarragon

1 cup sliced spring alliums, such as green garlic, green onions, or ramps

4 ounces freshly grated Pecorino Romano cheese

3/4 cup roasted hazelnuts (see page 24)

2 teaspoon kosher salt

3/4 cup extra virgin olive oil

In a food processor, blitz the herbs, alliums, cheese, hazelnuts, and salt until finely minced. With the motor on, slowly drizzle in the oil through the chute until a rough-textured pesto is achieved. Taste for seasoning and adjust as needed. The sauce will keep in an airtight container in the refrigerator for up to 3 days. Bring to room temperature before serving.

HERBY WALNUT SAUCE

Makes about 1 1/2 cups

This chunky nut-based sauce is a textured topping for roasted root vegetables and warm winter soups.

1 cup chopped roasted walnuts (see page 24)

1/4 cup grated Parmigiano-Reggiano cheese

1/4 cup chopped fresh flat-leaf parsley

2 tablespoons chopped fennel fronds (optional)

1 tablespoon chopped fresh rosemary leaves

1 tablespoon chopped fresh marjoram leaves

2 cloves garlic, minced

1 teaspoon Meyer lemon zest

1/2 teaspoon kosher salt

1/2 cup extra virgin olive oil

In a medium bowl, mix the walnuts, cheese, parsley, fennel fronds (if using), rosemary, marjoram, garlic, lemon zest, and salt. Drizzle in the olive oil and stir until well combined. The sauce will keep in an airtight container in the refrigerator for up to 3 days. Bring to room temperature before serving.

PISTACHIO ROMESCO

Makes about 2 cups

I use pistachios instead of almonds in this riff on the iconic Spanish sauce and add hot chiles to give it an extra kick.

1 dried guajillo chile

1 dried chipotle chile

1 medium tomato

1 large or 2 small sweet red peppers

¼ cup extra virgin olive oil

1 small red onion, diced

1 fresno or jalapeño chile, seeded and chopped

2 cloves garlic, sliced

2 teaspoons kosher salt

1 cup roasted pistachios

2 tablespoons sherry vinegar

Position an oven rack about 6 inches below the broiler and turn the broiler to high. Place the guajillo and chipotle chiles in a small bowl and cover them with boiling water. Let sit until ready to use.

Place the tomato and sweet pepper on a rimmed baking sheet. Broil, turning occasionally. When the tomato skin starts to split, remove from the oven and set aside to cool. The pepper may need a little longer; the goal is to completely char the skin. When the skin is evenly blackened, place the pepper in a bowl and cover with plastic film. Let sit for 10 minutes to steam.

Using your fingers or a paring knife, pull or scrape away the charred pepper skin. Remove the seeds, then coarsely chop the flesh. Peel away the skin of the tomato, then coarsely chop it.

Pour the olive oil into a wide skillet over medium heat. Add the onions, fresno or jalapeño chile, garlic, and 1 teaspoon of the salt and cook until the onions are translucent, about 5 minutes.

Meanwhile, remove the reconstituted chiles from the water and coarsely chop them. Add the chopped reconstituted chiles, roasted peppers, and tomatoes to the contents in the skillet and cook for 2 to 3 minutes. Add the pistachios, vinegar, and remaining salt and cook for another 2 to 3 minutes, stirring frequently. Transfer the mixture to a food processor and puree; the texture should be slightly chunky, which is desirable for this recipe. Taste for seasoning and adjust as needed. The sauce will keep in an airtight container in the refrigerator for up to 3 days. Bring to room temperature before serving.

SAUCE VIERGE

Makes about 2 cups

Michel Guérard is credited for creating this herb-laden tomato vinaigrette at a spa resort in France in the 1970s. It's everything you want out of a summer tomato sauce: fresh, light, and tangy, with no cooking involved.

1 large ripe beefsteak or oxheart tomato, cored and diced

1/3 cup extra virgin olive oil

1/3 cup chopped mixed fresh tender herbs, such as parsley, cilantro, tarragon, chervil, mint, and chives

2 tablespoons minced shallots

2 tablespoons fresh lemon juice

1 1/2 teaspoons kosher salt

In a medium bowl, mix the tomato, oil, herbs, shallots, lemon juice, and salt. Taste for seasoning and adjust as needed. This sauce is best served at room temperature on the day it is made.

VEGAN WALNUT BÉCHAMEL

Makes about 1 1/2 cups

A delicious nondairy, gluten-free interpretation of béchamel for my friends on a restricted diet.

1 tablespoon extra virgin olive oil

1 small leek, white and little green parts only, halved lengthwise and thinly sliced

1 cup walnuts

1 1/2 teaspoons kosher salt

1 teaspoon chopped fresh rosemary

1/2 teaspoon apple cider vinegar

1/2 teaspoon honey

Heat the oil in a medium skillet over medium heat. Add the leek, walnuts, salt, and rosemary and cook until the leeks are tender and the walnuts are toasted, 5 to 6 minutes, stirring often. Add 1 cup of water and stir well, scraping up the brown bits from the bottom of the pan. Bring the mixture to a simmer, then decrease the heat, cover with a lid, and cook for 8 to 10 minutes. Transfer the walnut mixture to a blender and blend with the vinegar and honey. If the mixture seems too thick or is not moving easily in the blender, add a little more water until desired consistency is achieved. It should be thick, creamy, and smooth when finished. Taste for seasoning and adjust as needed.

PART II

Recipes

ROOTS

Roots are the underground dwellers of the produce world. Because they grow beneath the soil, they each have protective skins and dense, firm flesh with earthy sweet flavors. For these reasons, roots can be treated similarly in the kitchen.

We commonly think of root vegetables as fall and winter produce meant for the roasting pan, but there are other paths. Try thinly shaving raw beets for a salad; spiralizing celery root into noodles; grilling whole carrots and turnips; or turning the sweetest ones, like sweet potatoes and parsnips, into desserts.

I tend to think about root vegetables as three distinct categories for cooking purposes: sweeter ones, starchier ones, and those with a higher moisture content. Sweet potatoes are great for pies and custards, and we know grated carrots give texture and flavor to cakes, but parsnips also have the same effect. The starchy bunch—celery root, mature turnips, rutabagas, and sunchokes—make velvety soups and purees, but also yield a creamy interior when roasted or braised. Those with a higher water content, like tender radishes and baby turnips, bring a snappy texture when served raw for snacking or in salads, but turn juicy when gently grilled or high-heat roasted.

While we tend to partner all roots with rich, deep flavors, they can also be complemented by vibrant vinaigrettes, tangy fresh cheeses, and bright citrus. Many of the roots have edible tops too. Turnips, carrots, beets, and radishes are often sold with their leaves attached, an added bonus to your wallet and your plate. Root vegetables are diverse in shape and size and they come in all colors and from all parts of the world. I've highlighted my favorites to cook with here from this vast vegetable category.

GINGERED CARROT BISQUE

Makes 6 to 8 servings

You know those carrots that look like they were maybe forgotten in the field and got really big? That's the kind I like to use here. They have a earthy sweetness that gives body and depth to this soup laced with hints of ginger, lime, star anise, and clove. Garnish with a little cultured dairy to add some tang against the mellow spiced flavor.

1½ pounds carrots, tops trimmed

4 tablespoons unsalted butter

1 yellow onion, chopped

4 cloves garlic, chopped

1 (2-inch) piece fresh ginger, peeled and thinly sliced

1 jalapeño or serrano chile, sliced

2 tablespoons kosher salt

1 whole clove

1 whole star anise

½ teaspoon freshly ground black pepper

7 cups Seasonal Vegetable Stock or Roasted Chicken Stock (page 11), or store-bought is fine, plus more as needed

1 to 2 tablespoons lime juice, plus zest of 1 small lime

1 to 2 tablespoons honey

½ cup plain kefir, or plain yogurt (not Greek) thinned with milk to a pourable consistency

Scrub the carrots with a vegetable brush under running water, then dry them with a kitchen towel. Peel the carrots only if their skins are too rough or dirty. Cut them crosswise into thick slices.

In a 6-quart Dutch oven, melt the butter over medium-high heat. Add the onions, garlic, ginger, chile, and salt. Cook, stirring often, until the onions are translucent, 6 to 8 minutes. Add the carrots, clove, star anise, and pepper and cook 5 minutes more, stirring often. Add the stock and bring to a simmer. Adjust the heat to maintain a gentle simmer and cook until the carrots are very tender, 20 to 25 minutes.

Puree the soup in a blender in two batches until velvety smooth. If it is too thick, thin it with a little more stock or water. Add 1 tablespoon lime juice and 1 tablespoon honey. Taste for seasoning, and add more lime juice, honey, or salt as needed. The flavor should be a little sweet, a little tangy, and fragrant from the spices and aromatics. Serve in warm bowls topped with a drizzle of kefir and sprinkle of lime zest.

GRILLED CARROTS WITH CARROT TOP CHERMOULA

Makes 4 servings

Grilling carrots whole creates a deliciously charred skin and a satisfying meaty texture while retaining their bright color inside. This recipe is ideal for those teenage carrots that are sold bunched with green tops attached. North African chermoula sauce adds a charming zing to the smoky grilled carrots, and it's a great opportunity to use the carrot tops instead of tossing them into the compost bin.

1 large bunch carrots with fresh green tops attached

1 tablespoon extra virgin olive oil

1 teaspoon fine sea salt

1 recipe Carrot Top Chermoula (page 40)

Heat the grill. If using gas, set to medium-high. If cooking over wood or charcoal, allow the flames to die down until the embers are glowing. If using a grill pan, place it over medium-high heat just before cooking.

Trim and reserve the tops from the carrots to make the chermoula. Scrub the carrots with a vegetable brush under running water, then wipe them clean with a kitchen towel. If any of the carrots are more than 1 inch in diameter, cut them in half lengthwise, but leave thinner carrots whole. Place the carrots in a shallow dish, rub them with the oil, and sprinkle with the salt.

Place the carrots on the hot grill, arranging them perpendicular to the grates so they don't fall through. (If you're using a grill pan, cook in batches and place a heavy skillet on top of the carrots to weigh them down while cooking.) Cook, turning occasionally, until nicely charred on all sides, 12 to 15 minutes. Transfer the grilled carrots back to the dish. Once cool enough to handle, cut the carrots into about 2-inch pieces. I like to slice the tapered end of the carrot away at a 90-degree angle then bisect the top half through the stem end, to get three pieces that are close to the same length and width, but use your best judgment based on the size of each carrot.

Arrange the carrots on a platter and spoon the chermoula over them. Serve warm or at room temperature, with any remaining chermoula on the side.

SLOW-COOKED LAMB AND RUTABAGA STEW

Makes 6 to 8 servings

Put this one-pot braise in your oven on a Sunday afternoon and your kitchen will soon be filled with an intoxicating aroma. Cooking at a low temperature tenderizes the cold-weather rutabagas and lamb shoulder simultaneously. Ask your butcher to tie the roast for even cooking and a tidy presentation. I like to serve this dish with my Salsa Verde recipe (page 39) and enjoy it with a deep, fruity red wine like Syrah or Cabernet, with some crusty bread to sop up the fragrant braising liquid.

One 4- to 5-pound boneless lamb shoulder roast, tied

2 tablespoons kosher salt

2 teaspoons freshly ground black pepper

4 tablespoons Ras el Hanout (page 5), or store-bought is fine

2 pounds rutabagas

2 tablespoon extra virgin olive oil

2 yellow onions, cut into 1-inch dice

5 cloves garlic, chopped

1½ cups dry white wine

4 cups Seasonal Vegetable Stock or Roasted Chicken Stock (page 11), or store-bought, water, or a combination is fine

5 bay leaves

One 1-inch piece of fresh ginger, peeled and sliced

1 orange, quartered and seeds removed

Fresh parsley and mint leaves for garnish

Heat the oven to 325ºF. Place the lamb shoulder in a baking dish and sprinkle 1 tablespoon of the salt all over the outer surface of the meat. Repeat with the black pepper and 2 tablespoons of the ras el hanout. On a cutting board, trim and peel the rutabagas and cut them into 1-inch cubes; set aside.

Place a Dutch oven over medium heat and add the oil. When the oil is shimmering, gently place the lamb in the Dutch oven and cook on all sides until the exterior is browned and a nice fond (those browned bits stuck to the bottom of the pot) forms, 8 to 10 minutes. Transfer the lamb back to the baking dish. Immediately add the onions and garlic, and the remaining 1 tablespoon salt to the pot. Using a wooden spoon, vigorously stir the onion mixture while scraping the fond from the bottom of the pot to prevent the spices from burning. Add the remaining ras el hanout and continue stirring. Cook until the spices are aromatic and the onions begin to soften, about 2 minutes, then add the wine and broth or water. Continue stirring to make sure all the fond has been freed from the bottom of the pot, then add the rutabagas, bay leaves, and ginger. Squeeze the orange pieces over the pot, then drop the rinds directly into the liquid and stir to combine. Carefully lower the lamb back into the pot along with any juices or spices that have settled in the dish. Bring the liquid to a simmer, then place a lid on the Dutch oven and transfer it to the oven.

Braise for 2 hours, then remove the lid and continue to cook for 30 to 40 more minutes until the top of the lamb is nicely browned and the liquid has reduced a bit. Carefully remove the pot from the oven and set aside to cool for a few minutes.

Remove the lamb from the braise with a long spatula wedged underneath and tongs gripping the sides of the meat for support. Place the meat on a carving board (preferably one with a moat for collecting the juices). Skim the excess fat from the top of the braising liquid and discard the orange rinds and bay leaves. Taste a rutabaga for doneness and the braising liquid for seasoning. The rutabagas should be tender and flavorful and the liquid well seasoned, so add more salt to your liking.

Snip the butcher's twine to untie the lamb and cut it into thick slices. Spoon the rutabaga mixture and some of the braising liquid into large shallow bowls and place a slice of lamb alongside each serving. Garnish each with a handful of fresh herbs.

ROASTED SWEET POTATOES WITH SEAWEED-CHILE BUTTER

Makes 4 to 6 servings

I once collaborated on a vegetable-themed dinner with some chef friends, and we came up with this unexpected idea for sweet potatoes. It has dried seaweed worked into a compound butter for a deep umami flavor, smoky chiles for a kick of heat, and lots of zingy lime. When the butter melts onto the surface of the sweet potato, all of these ingredients work together to form a complexity that fires on all cylinders.

2 ½ pounds sweet potatoes, scrubbed

1 recipe Seaweed-Chile Butter (page 35)

Flaky sea salt for garnish

Heat the oven to 400°F. Place the sweet potatoes on a baking sheet lined with parchment paper or aluminum foil and roast until they are just tender when pierced in the center with a paring knife, 40 to 60 minutes, depending on their size. When they are close to being done, they may begin to release some of their syrup. It's important to remove them from the oven before they are too mushy, so they hold their shape when sliced. Let the sweet potatoes cool briefly.

Once the sweet potatoes are cool enough to handle, cut them crosswise into ½-inch disks, keeping the skins intact as best as you can. Arrange the warm sweet potato disks on a serving platter and top each with a dollop of the seaweed butter. Sprinkle with flaky sea salt and serve warm.

SWEET POTATO CUSTARDS

Makes 6 servings

The classic French spice blend quatre épices is like a more sophisticated version of pumpkin pie spice, and it works perfectly with sweet fall produce. In this case the sweet potato is the star. The crystallized ginger and cool crème fraîche are not only beautiful garnishes but add depth and dimension as finishing touches. If you serve these at your holiday gathering, they will quickly end up on next year's request list.

1¼ pounds garnet sweet potatoes

1 tablespoon unsalted butter

2 large eggs, beaten until frothy

½ cup granulated sugar

1½ teaspoons Quatre Épices (page 6), or store-bought is fine

½ teaspoon kosher salt

1 cup half-and-half, or ½ cup heavy cream plus ½ cup whole milk

¼ cup fresh orange juice, plus ½ teaspoon finely grated orange zest

1 teaspoon pure vanilla extract

Crème fraîche for garnish

Sliced crystallized ginger for garnish

Heat the oven to 400ºF with a rack in the center. Place the sweet potatoes in a baking dish and roast until they are very tender when pierced in the center with a paring knife, 45 to 60 minutes, depending on their size. When the potatoes are cool enough to handle, remove the skins and place the flesh in a mixing bowl. Mash the sweet potatoes with a potato masher or fork. Set aside 1½ cups of the mash and reserve any remaining for another use.

Grease six 8-ounce ramekins with the butter.

Add the beaten eggs, sugar, quatre épices, and salt to the sweet potatoes and whisk until fully combined. Add the half-and-half, orange juice and zest, and vanilla and whisk to combine.

Pour the custard mixture into the prepared ramekins, dividing it evenly. Place the ramekins in a deep roasting pan spaced 1 to 2 inches apart. Pour in enough hot water to come halfway up the sides of the ramekins. Carefully transfer the roasting pan to the oven and bake until the custards are set but still just a little jiggly in the center, 18 to 22 minutes.

Carefully remove the roasting pan from the oven. Transfer the ramekins from the water bath to a cooling rack and cool completely. (The cooled custards can be wrapped tightly in plastic film and refrigerated for up to 1 day. Bring to room temperature before serving.)

Serve the custards topped with a dollop of crème fraîche and some sliced crystallized ginger.

FRAGRANT BEETS AND CHERRIES WITH CASHEW BUTTER

Makes 6 servings

When I roast beets, I like to impart interesting flavors to brighten or complement the natural earthiness of this deeply hued root. Chamomile and hibiscus infuse floral notes into this dish, while the vinegar adds a tart, fruity dimension. I'm fond of the tearing method for cooked beets, which creates nooks and crannies for catching the creamy cashew butter.

1½ pounds red beets, stems and root ends trimmed

¾ cup red wine vinegar

⅓ cup dried hibiscus flowers

3 tablespoons dried chamomile

3 tablespoons extra virgin olive oil, plus more for drizzling

2 tablespoons plus ½ teaspoon kosher salt

½ cup unsweetened cashew butter

1 tablespoon fresh lemon juice, plus more to finish

½ pound cherries, pitted and torn into halves

½ cup coarsely chopped roasted cashews (see page 24)

Flaky sea salt

Freshly ground black pepper

Mint leaves and/or edible flowers

Heat the oven to 375ºF. Place the beets in a deep baking dish that is large enough so they can snugly fit in one layer. In a small bowl, whisk the vinegar, hibiscus, chamomile, olive oil, and 2 tablespoons of the salt. Pour the mixture over the beets. Cover with a sheet of parchment paper and then foil, and cinch the foil around the edges to make a tight seal to steam-roast the beets. Place the baking dish in the oven.

After 1 hour, remove the parchment and foil and test the doneness of the beets by piercing each one with the tip of a paring knife. If they still feel firm, re-cover and return the dish to the oven, adding a splash of water if any liquid evaporated. Continue checking for doneness every 20 minutes or so. For smaller beets, the cook time is about 1 hour, medium-size beets take around 90 minutes, and large beets up to 2 hours. When finished, turn each beet over so that the side that was facing up is now facing down in the liquid and let cool. (This will help ensure even peeling by hydrating the skin on both sides.)

Don a pair of disposable gloves if you have them, to protect your hands from staining, and wipe away the skins of the beets using a paper towel. (They should come off easily, but if they don't, you can use a paring knife to remove any stubborn clinging skin.) Once the beets are peeled and cooled, and while still wearing the gloves, tear them into bite-size pieces using your fingers, creating craggy edges that will later soak up the cashew butter. Place the beets in a bowl and discard the skins and cooking liquid.

In a medium bowl, combine the cashew butter with the remaining ½ teaspoon salt, the lemon juice, and 2 tablespoons of water. Whisk until the cashew butter absorbs the liquids and continue adding 1 tablespoon of water at a time until it becomes thinner and easily spreadable. Taste for seasoning and adjust to your liking.

Spread the cashew sauce on a serving platter and pile the beets and cherries on top. Squeeze a little more lemon juice over everything and drizzle with more olive oil. Top with chopped cashews, sea salt, pepper, and mint or flowers.

GOLDEN BEETS WITH SIZZLING BEET TOPS

Makes 4 servings

My goal is to always use every part of the plant, and beets are a prime example. In this recipe, golden beets are diced small and cooked quickly in a stir-fry-inspired preparation, then their greens are wilted in. The dish is completed with a contrasting crunch from sesame seeds and crushed peanuts. There is just the right amount of Szechuan peppercorns to create that warm, sizzling feeling on your tongue.

1 bunch golden beets with healthy tops (about 2 pounds)

3 tablespoons peanut oil

1 tablespoon kosher salt

2 tablespoons minced shallots

1 tablespoon minced ginger

1 tablespoon minced garlic

½ teaspoon Szechuan peppercorns or freshly cracked black peppercorns

¼ cup chopped roasted peanuts (see page 24)

2 tablespoons toasted sesame seeds

1 teaspoon fresh lemon or lime juice

1 tablespoon chopped shiso or mint leaves

Slice the beet tops from the roots and wash the tops well under cold running water. Shake them off and place on a cutting board. Thinly slice the stems crosswise and coarsely chop the greens. Place them in a bowl and set aside. Peel the beetroots and cut them into ¼-inch cubes.

Place a cast-iron skillet over medium heat. Add 2 tablespoons of the oil and heat until shimmering. Add the diced beets and season with 1½ teaspoons of the salt. Cook, stirring often, until the beets just become tender, 7 to 8 minutes. Transfer the beets to a bowl using a slotted spoon and set aside.

Add the remaining tablespoon of oil to the pan, then the beet greens and chopped stems, shallots, ginger, garlic, peppercorns, and remaining 1½ teaspoons of salt. Cook, stirring almost constantly, until the greens are wilted, 3 to 4 minutes. Add the peanuts, sesame seeds, and cooked beetroots and stir well. Turn the heat off and add the citrus juice. Taste for seasoning and adjust as needed. Garnish with shiso or mint leaves and serve directly from the pan.

SPICED PARSNIP CAKE WITH LEMON GLAZE

Makes 12 to 16 servings

Make this cake at Christmastime and keep it on the counter for family to enjoy with afternoon tea, or alongside some boozy eggnog by the fire. Grated parsnip in the batter keeps the cake extra moist and forms a foundation of flavor enhanced by holiday spices.

CAKE

1½ cups canola oil, plus more for greasing

2½ cups unbleached all-purpose flour, plus more for dusting

1¼ teaspoons baking powder

1 teaspoon baking soda

1 teaspoon freshly ground black pepper

1 teaspoon ground cinnamon

1 teaspoon ground ginger

½ teaspoon ground cardamom

½ teaspoon freshly grated nutmeg

½ teaspoon fine sea salt

⅛ teaspoon ground clove

1¼ pounds parsnips

4 large eggs

1½ cups granulated sugar

½ cup light brown sugar

GLAZE

1¾ cups confectioner's sugar, plus more as needed

¼ teaspoon fine sea salt

2 tablespoons buttermilk, plus more as needed

2 tablespoons fresh lemon juice, plus 1 teaspoon finely grated lemon zest

TO MAKE THE CAKE: Heat the oven to 350°F with a rack in the center. Lightly grease a 10-inch (12-cup) Bundt pan with oil or nonstick spray, making sure to get into each crevice. Dust evenly with some flour, then turn the pan upside down and tap out the excess. Set aside.

In a medium bowl, whisk the flour, baking powder, baking soda, pepper, cinnamon, ginger, cardamom, nutmeg, salt, and clove. Set the dry mix aside.

Trim, peel, and grate the parsnips on the largest holes of a box grater.

In a stand mixer fitted with the paddle attachment, or in a large mixing bowl using a handheld electric mixer, beat the eggs, oil, and both sugars until fully combined. With the mixer on low speed or by hand with a wooden spoon, alternate stirring in the dry mix and grated parsnips in 3 batches each. Stop stirring once the dry mix is fully moistened to avoid overworking the batter to keep the cake tender.

Transfer the batter to the prepared Bundt pan and bake until a cake tester or toothpick comes out clean, about 55 minutes. Set the cake on a cooling rack for about 10 minutes. Then invert the pan to unmold the cake onto the rack and cool completely.

TO MAKE THE GLAZE: Sift the confectioner's sugar and salt into a medium bowl. Add the buttermilk and lemon juice and zest, and whisk until completely smooth. The consistency of the glaze should resemble school glue (but with a sweet, lemony flavor!). Adjust consistency by adding more buttermilk or confectioner's sugar as needed.

Drizzle the glaze over the cooled cake and allow it to set for at least 20 minutes before cutting and serving. (The cake can be made up to 1 day ahead; store, covered, at room temperature.)

BUTTERY ROASTED PARSNIPS WITH MOLE CRUNCH

Makes 4 to 6 servings

Parsnips have a high starch content and a tough inner core that requires tenderizing before roasting. My solution: I cut them into wedges and blanch them in water before they go in the oven. After roasting in melted butter, the result is a sweet, caramelized exterior and soft, creamy center. They are fantastic on their own as oven fries, but I especially love them sprinkled with my Mole Crunch topping when they are hot out of the oven.

¼ cup kosher salt

2 pounds parsnips

4 tablespoons unsalted butter, at room temperature

½ cup Mole Crunch (page 27)

Heat the oven to 425ºF. Place racks in the center and top positions in the oven. Bring 3 quarts of water to a boil over high heat and add the salt.

Place the parsnips on a cutting board, then trim the ends and peel the skins. Cut each parsnip in half crosswise where they begin to dramatically taper. Using the narrower bottom half as your guide, cut the top half lengthwise into sticks that match the thickness of the bottom half.

Place the parsnips in the boiling salted water and cook until the water returns to a lively simmer and the parsnips are still a little firm but pliable, 4 to 6 minutes. Drain the parsnips well in a colander and return them to the dry pot. Add the butter in chunks and toss well to melt it and evenly coat the parsnips. Spread them on a large rimmed baking sheet and roast on the center rack of the oven until the parsnips are tender and caramelized on the bottom, about 15 minutes. If you'd like more caramelization, switch the oven to broil on high and cook for 2 to 4 minutes until the desired color is achieved. Pile the hot parsnips on a serving platter and sprinkle with the mole crunch.

CELERY ROOT NOODLES WITH SMOKED TROUT AND BEURRE BLANC

Makes 4 servings

This dish was developed by Mykel Burkhart, chef de cuisine at Miller Union, as a lunch entrée for the winter months. Hard, knotty celery root is peeled and spiralized into fettuccine-like noodles then lightly blanched and tossed with smoked trout and an aromatic butter sauce. It was wildly popular with our lunch crowd and will surely become one of your favorite cold-weather meals.

3 pounds celery root

¼ cup kosher salt

1 recipe Beurre Blanc sauce (page 38)

6 ounces smoked trout filets, skin discarded, flaked into large bite-size pieces

1 cup coarsely chopped fresh dill, fennel fronds, or a combination

Lemon wedges for serving

Bring 1 gallon of water to a boil in a large pot. Place a colander in the sink.

Place the celery root on a cutting board and slice off the stem end, opposite the knotty side. With the cut side flat on the cutting board, carve away the rough skin and knots with a knife, then clean up any edges with a peeler to fully expose the flesh. One at a time, attach each root to a spiralizer and process to make flat noodles that resemble fettuccine. (If your spiralizer only makes one shape of noodle, that is fine, but note that thinner noodles may take less time to cook.)

Season the boiling water with the salt and add the celery root noodles. Cook until the noodles are al dente, about 1 minute. Watch them closely and be careful to avoid overcooking; you're really just looking to take away the rawness while keeping the noodles intact, as they are delicate and break apart easily. Immediately drain the noodles in the colander and shake gently to dry them well. Transfer the noodles back to the pot and gently toss with the beurre blanc, smoked trout, and about half of the herbs. Divide the noodles among warm plates or bowls, top with more herbs, and serve with lemon wedges on the side.

SILKY CELERY ROOT SOUP

Makes 4 to 6 servings

Starchy vegetables, like celery root, can be cooked until tender and blended to create a silky soup that feels and tastes creamy without actually using cream. To keep this dairy-free, use chicken schmaltz instead of butter, which also adds a rich poultry undertone.

2 pounds celery root

1 leek

¼ cup schmaltz or unsalted butter

1 cup chopped celery

1 cup diced fennel

1 tart apple like Granny Smith or Pink Lady, quartered, cored, and chopped

2 cloves garlic, chopped

4 teaspoons sea salt

1 quart Roasted Chicken Stock (page 11), or store-bought is fine

Herby Walnut Sauce (page 41) for garnish

Place the celery root on a cutting board and slice off the stem end, opposite the knotty side. With the cut side flat on the cutting board, carve away the rough skin and knots with a knife, then clean up any edges with a peeler to fully expose the flesh. Cut the celery root into 3/4-inch chunks.

Trim the root end and dark green tops from the leek, saving the tops for your next batch of stock (see page 10). Cut the leek in half lengthwise and thinly slice each half crosswise. Place the sliced leeks in a bowl and cover with water. Vigorously agitate the leeks to release any sand or dirt between the layers. Let sit for a few minutes; the leeks will float to the top and the dirt will settle at the bottom of the bowl. Skim the leeks from the top of the water and place them in a colander to drain well.

In a medium Dutch oven, melt the schmaltz or butter over medium-high heat. Add the leek, celery, fennel, apple, garlic, and salt. Cook, stirring often, until everything is beginning to soften, 4 to 5 minutes. Add the celery root and chicken stock and bring to a simmer. Adjust the heat to maintain a gentle simmer and cook until the celery root is very tender, 20 to 25 minutes.

Puree the soup in a blender in two batches until velvety smooth. If it is too thick, thin it with a little more stock or water. Taste for seasoning and adjust to your liking. Serve in warm bowls, topped with the herby walnut sauce.

EVERYTHING RADISHES

Makes 12 to 16

Radishes eaten with butter and salt are an iconic French pairing of simple perfection, and a starting point of inspiration for this dish. At Miller Union, we serve radishes with a dip of salty crumbled feta bathed in buttermilk. But this combination takes it to the next level. The radishes are coated in creamy chèvre, and then rolled in "everything" bagel seasoning for a fun new take on an old classic. *See image on page iv-v*

2 bunches radishes, such as French Breakfast, Cherry Belle, or other crisp-tender varieties

4 ounces chèvre

1 to 3 tablespoons plain kefir or buttermilk

1 recipe Everything Seasoning (page 27)

If the radishes have tops and they look healthy, leave them attached. Wash the radishes in a large bowl of cool water, gently scrubbing them to remove any dirt, especially around the stem end. Drain and wrap the radishes in paper towels to dry.

Crumble the chèvre into a medium bowl and add 1 tablespoon kefir or buttermilk. Whisk, adding more of the liquid as needed, until the mixture is smooth and spreadable. Pour the everything seasoning into a loose pile in a shallow bowl. One at a time, drag each radish through the whipped chèvre to coat well, then roll in the seasoning blend. Place the radishes on a platter as they are coated. Serve immediately or cover and refrigerate for up to 8 hours.

CONFETTI SALAD

Makes 4 to 6 servings

When you've lost inspiration for a healthy meal in January, turn to rainbow-colored radishes, carrots, and beets to nix the doldrums. It's also a great way to hone your knife skills. Shave and cut the winter roots into thin batons for a fresh, crunchy lunch.

2 pounds mixed root vegetables, such as watermelon radish, daikon radish, golden or chioggia beets, and carrots

1 tart-sweet apple, such as honeycrisp, pink lady, or Fuji

2 tablespoons apple cider vinegar

2 tablespoons sunflower or grapeseed oil

1 jalapeño chile, minced

2 teaspoons coarse sea salt

1/4 cup mixed chopped tender herbs such as parsley, dill, chervil, chive, mint, and tarragon

1/4 cup roasted sunflower seeds (see page 24)

1/4 cup crumbled goat's milk feta cheese

Scrub the skins of the roots and apple and remove any traces of dirt. Peel the skins of the roots if they are weathered, thick, or too fibrous, but otherwise leave them intact. Cut each root into matchsticks (julienne) using a mandoline, a food processor with julienne attachment, or a sharp chef's knife. Core the apple and cut it into matchsticks the same way.

Place the roots and apple in a large mixing bowl, add the vinegar, oil, jalapeño, and salt, and toss well to coat. Add the herbs and gently toss again. Taste for seasoning and adjust to your liking. Transfer the salad to a large serving bowl and top with the sunflower seeds and feta.

CARAMELIZED SUNCHOKES AND MEYER LEMONS

Makes 4 to 6 servings

Deeply roasting sunchokes intensifies their nutty flavor. The caramelized skins become pleasantly sticky between the teeth, and the soft flesh soaks up the lemon-scented olive oil.

2 pounds sunchokes

2 Meyer lemons

3/4 cup extra virgin olive oil

1 tablespoon kosher salt

Heat the oven to 425ºF with a rack in the center. Scrub the sunchokes with a vegetable brush under running water, then wipe them clean with a kitchen towel. Cut them into bite-size pieces. Since their sizes may vary, some might be cut in half, while others need to be cut into multiple pieces. Because of their natural knobby shape, the pieces will be irregular, but aim for similar sizes so they roast evenly. Place the cut sunchokes in a large bowl.

Trim the ends from the lemons then slice them in half lengthwise. Place the halves cut side down on the cutting board, and slice them crosswise into thin half-moons. Remove any seeds from the slices, then add them to the bowl with the sunchokes. Add the oil and salt and toss well to coat.

Turn the sunchokes and lemons out onto a large rimmed baking sheet. Olive oil will pool in the pan, which is a good thing as it makes the sunchokes really tender and helps them caramelize. Roast until the sunchokes are very tender with some nice browning at the edges and the lemons are browned too, about 30 minutes, rotating the pan in the oven halfway through. If you'd like more caramelization, switch the oven to broil on high and cook for 2 to 4 minutes until the desired color is achieved.

GRILLED HAKUREI TURNIPS WITH MISO VINAIGRETTE

Makes 4 servings

This technique is inspired by Japanese grilling. After building a ripping-hot fire in a charcoal grill, push the coals to one side to divide the grill into two zones: a hot side and a cooler side. It doesn't take long to grill the roots over the glowing embers, while the green tops are positioned over the cooler side to cook more gently. The result is juicy charred turnips with smoky wilted greens that are crisp and browned at the edges. The contrasting textures are dynamic.

1 large bunch hakurei turnips with healthy tops

Canola or other neutral oil

1 teaspoon kosher salt

½ teaspoon freshly ground black pepper

1 recipe Miso Vinaigrette (page 20)

Heat the grill. If using gas, set to high. If cooking over wood or charcoal, allow the flames to die down until the embers are glowing.

Wash the turnip roots and attached greens in a large bowl of cool water, gently scrubbing them to remove any dirt, especially around the base of the stems. Drain and wrap them in paper towels to dry.

Cut the turnip roots in half lengthwise through the stems to get 2 halves with tops attached to each. Place the turnips on a large tray and drizzle with enough oil to lightly coat them. Season with salt and pepper and set aside.

Just before cooking, create two heat zones on your grill by turning off the heating elements on one half of a gas grill or banking the hot coals to one side of a charcoal grill.

Position the turnips on the grill with cut sides down over the hot part of the grill, and the tops draped over the grates on the cooler side. Cover and cook until the roots have nice grill marks, 5 to 8 minutes. Turn the turnip roots and greens to cook on the other side until the roots are just tender, juicy, and lightly charred and the greens are wilted and charred in some places, 5 to 8 minutes more.

Pile the turnips on a serving platter and spoon some of the miso vinaigrette over the top. Serve the remaining vinaigrette on the side.

ROAST CHICKEN AND TURNIP TRAY BAKE

Makes 4 to 6 servings

The British-coined term "tray bake" succinctly summarizes the ease of using one baking sheet to make a meal. Everything is tossed and roasted together, making cleanup a breeze. I particularly like how the turnips and pears become visually indiscernible: The only way to tell them apart is by taste. The rosemary and citrus add high notes to this earthy, wintry dish. A simple green salad, to me, is the perfect accompaniment.

1½ pounds purple-top turnips

2 ripe Bosc pears, halved and cored

1 yellow onion

2 tablespoons extra virgin olive oil

2 tablespoons rosemary needles

Zest of 1 orange

Zest of 1 lemon

1 tablespoon kosher salt

1 teaspoon freshly ground black pepper

6 bone-in, skin-on chicken thighs

Heat the oven to 425ºF with a rack in the center. Peel the turnips, then slice them in half through the stem end and place each half cut side down. Trim away any tough pieces from the top and bottom. Cut the turnips into wedges that are 1 inch wide on the outer edge. Place the turnip wedges on a large rimmed baking sheet.

Cut the pears and onion into wedges about the same width as the turnips and add them to the baking sheet. Add the oil, rosemary, orange and lemon zest, 1½ teaspoons of the salt, and ½ teaspoon of the pepper and toss it all together. Spread the mixture in an even layer to the edges of the pan.

Season the chicken thighs with the remaining 1½ teaspoons salt and ½ teaspoon pepper and arrange them over the turnip mixture, evenly spaced. Pick out some of the rosemary and place it over the chicken skin.

Place the sheet pan in the oven and roast until the center of each chicken thigh registers 170ºF on an instant-read thermometer and the vegetables and pears are tender, 45 to 50 minutes. Serve directly from the pan, making sure to spoon up the juices that collect on the bottom.

LEAVES

When I look outside and see greenery everywhere, I am reminded of the vitality of our natural surroundings. This life force is present in all plants, and perhaps there is no better visual representation than in healthy green leaves. A complete day for me includes integrating that greenery into nourishment. In fact, if I don't incorporate something green into my daily meals, I feel like I have missed the mark. This chapter has a special meaning for me, and I want to share some of the ways that greens inspire me.

On the palate, leaves can be divided into mild, bitter, or peppery. In the mild spectrum, lettuces like romaine and its cousin little gem are a blank canvas for building flavor. Moving up the dial, spinach, chard, and kale are also mild but with more distinctive flavors. Bitter leaves like dandelion, endive, escarole, and radicchio all possess that gripping bite that resonates on the back of the tongue. Peppery leaves, such as watercress, mustards, and arugula, are relatives of horseradish, so they carry a potent punch.

After considering taste, next comes texture. Tender-crisp leaves like lettuces, arugula, watercress, and baby greens are almost always served raw but can be wilted with a little heat for a luscious mouthfeel. Hardy greens like kale and collards are ideal for cooking to tenderize their sturdy structure but can be enjoyed raw when you slice them thinly. These greens often have tough stems, and I recommend that you separate them from the leaves and use them in stocks or for juicing, or finely chop them crosswise to sauté with onions and garlic as the base for whatever you're cooking.

Greens like spinach, chard, and mustards have tender leaves and crunchy, less fibrous stems, offering two delightful textures.

No matter the type, I find it easy to work greens into almost every meal. Throw a handful of arugula onto a tray of hot roasted vegetables and mix them in to wilt. Put some chopped lacinato kale in the colander before pouring in your pasta to drain, then toss with the steaming noodles. Sauté the brightly colored stems of rainbow chard as the base of a soup and add the leaves to the hot broth. I even go so far as to making pureed kale the base of my French toast batter—that's how much I like eating leafy greens.

THE NEW WEDGE SALAD

Makes 4 servings

A wedge of iceberg lettuce with crisp bacon and juicy tomatoes, drenched in blue cheese dressing, is a well-established American classic But I often want to change up a classic, taking it into new territory. Wedges of leafy romaine are a fresh starting point to add crunchy fried peas, pickled onions, and a creamy sun-dried tomato dressing that's reminiscent of Thousand Island, but better.

⅓ cup oil-packed sun-dried tomatoes, drained and chopped

1 large egg

2 tablespoons fresh lime juice

1 tablespoon apple cider vinegar

2 cloves garlic, finely minced or pressed

1 teaspoon chili powder

1 teaspoon kosher salt

¾ cup canola oil

½ cup buttermilk

2 small or 1 large head romaine lettuce, chilled

1 small cucumber

1 recipe Lime-Pickled Red Onions (page 30)

1 recipe Crunchy Fried Field Peas or Beans (page 26)

In a food processor, combine the sun-dried tomatoes, egg, lime juice, apple cider vinegar, garlic, chili powder, and salt and blitz to a coarse paste. With the motor running, slowly drizzle in the oil in a steady stream to emulsify. Stop and scrape down the sides and bottom of the bowl and blitz again. With the motor still running, pour in the buttermilk and process just to combine. Taste for seasoning. Chill the dressing in an airtight container until needed. (The dressing will keep in the refrigerator for up to 3 days.)

Cut the romaine lengthwise into halves (if using small heads) or quarters (if using one larger head). Using a mandoline or sharp chef's knife, slice the cucumber as thinly as possible.

Arrange one wedge of romaine on each plate with the cut sides up. Drizzle generously with the dressing, letting it fall between the leaves and form a little pool on the plate. Scatter the cucumbers, pickled onions, and crispy peas on top.

LITTLE GEMS WITH SPRING GODDESS DRESSING

Makes 4 to 6 servings

Little gems are a type of romaine crossed with butterhead lettuce. They grow to a cute dwarf size, and can be all green, bronze tipped, or reddish purple, depending on the variety. Despite their delicate nature, they are great when cut in half and grilled, or tossed with a robust vinaigrette. But here I separate the wispy leaves and drizzle them with a spring take on creamy green goddess dressing to highlight their ethereal quality.

½ cup chopped green garlic (white and green parts)

1 to 2 tablespoons fresh lime juice

1 tablespoon thinly sliced fresh chives

1 tablespoon chopped fresh dill

1 tablespoon chopped fresh parsley

1 tablespoon chopped fresh tarragon

½ teaspoon kosher salt

¾ cup Homemade Mayonnaise (page 14), or store-bought is fine

1½ pounds little gem lettuces

2 small or 1 medium carrot

4 hakurei turnips or radishes of your choice

In a food processor, pulse the green garlic, 1 tablespoon of lime juice, the chives, dill, parsley, tarragon, and salt until finely minced and combined. Add the mayonnaise and process until fully incorporated, scraping the sides of the bowl as needed. Taste for seasoning and add more lime juice to your liking. Chill the dressing in an airtight container until needed. (The dressing will keep in the refrigerator for up to 3 days.)

Trim the root end from each head of lettuce and separate the leaves. Fill a large bowl or your clean kitchen sink with water and submerge the lettuce. Pull the leaves out and place in a salad spinner, leaving the water, and any dirt that sinks to the bottom, behind. Spin dry and refrigerate until needed.

Using a mandoline or vegetable peeler, shave the carrots lengthwise into ribbons. Slice the turnips or radishes into rounds with a mandoline or sharp chef's knife.

Divide the chilled lettuce among serving plates and layer with the shaved carrots and turnips or radishes. Drizzle the top of each salad with some of the dressing and serve cold.

LUCK AND MONEY DOLMAS

Makes 8 to 12 servings; about 22 dolmas

If you're from the South, you know the tradition of ringing in the New Year with a celebratory meal centered around Hoppin' John and collard greens, representing good luck and prosperity in the year to come. With this ritual in mind, I concocted little party hors d'oeuvres inspired by Greek dolmas, but wrapped them with collards instead of grape leaves, and filled them with slow-simmered field peas and steamed rice.

1 cup dried black-eyed peas, crowder peas, or other dried field pea

2 tablespoons extra virgin olive oil

1 cup diced yellow onion

1 small jalapeño, finely chopped

1/4 cup plus 1 1/2 tablespoons kosher salt

3 sprigs thyme

22 medium-size collard green leaves (6 to 8 inches wide) or 11 larger collard green leaves

1 cup medium grain rice

1 tablespoon Louisiana-style hot sauce like Crystal, Texas Pete, or Louisiana brand, plus more for serving

1 tablespoon apple cider vinegar

Place the dried peas in a medium saucepan, cover with 2 to 3 inches of water, and set aside at room temperature overnight, or for at least 6 hours.

Drain the peas in a colander. Wipe out the saucepan and place it over medium heat. Add the olive oil, onions, and jalapeño and season with 1 teaspoon of the salt. Cook, stirring occasionally, until the onions are translucent, 4 to 5 minutes. Add the drained peas and thyme and cover with 4 cups of water. Bring to a lively simmer, then decrease the heat to maintain a gentle simmer and cook until the peas are tender, 1 to 1 1/2 hours, adding more water as needed to keep the peas submerged. Near the end of the cook time, when the peas are almost tender, add 1 tablespoon of the salt. When finished, the peas should be very tender but hold their shape, and the water in the pot will thicken a bit from the starch they released. Remove the pan from the heat and let the peas cool in the cooking liquid.

Place a 6-quart pot filled with 3 quarts of water over high heat and add 1/4 cup of the salt. Bring to a boil.

Rinse the collard greens under cool running water. Trim the stem at the base of each leaf. If working with larger, mature leaves (over 8 inches wide), halve them crosswise, perpendicular to the center stem. When the water reaches a boil, drop about half of the leaves in and use tongs or a slotted spoon to separate them. Cook until the leaves and center veins are tender, 3 to 8 minutes, depending on how thick and fibrous (mature) they are. Adjust the heat as needed to maintain a lively simmer. Remove the leaves with tongs as they are done and lay them out on paper towels in a single layer to cool. Repeat as needed until all the leaves are blanched. Pat the leaves dry with paper towels.

In a small saucepan, combine the rice with 2 cups of water and the remaining 1/2 teaspoon salt and bring to a boil over high heat. Decrease the heat to low, cover, and cook for 15 minutes. Remove the lid and fluff with a fork. Turn the rice out into a wide, shallow container and spread it out to cool.

Drain the cooled peas, reserving the cooking liquid, and discard the thyme sprigs. Add the peas to the container with the rice and mix them together. Stir in the hot sauce and vinegar. Add just enough of the pea cooking liquid to make the mixture moist, but you should be able to squeeze some together in the palm of your hand and it will hold its shape. Taste the filling and adjust the seasoning as needed.

Drop the rice and pea mixture by the spoonful into the center of each collard green leaf, using about 3 tablespoons per leaf and covering about a 2-inch-by-1-inch rectangular area. Roll the bottom of the leaf over the mixture, tucking in the sides as you round the filling, like you're rolling a burrito. When nicely wrapped and tucked, set the dolma down on the seam side and repeat until they are all filled. Serve at room temp or slightly chilled, along with extra hot sauce.

GREENS GRILLED CHEESE

Makes 2 large sandwiches; 4 servings

We served this sandwich as a vegetarian option when Miller Union was open for lunch, and you could often find me scarfing one down in the back between shifts. It's that kind of healthy-meets-decadent mash-up that I just can't resist. For the greens, I recommend chard, spinach, kale, mustards, or a mix. Note that the mayo is used to coat the outside of the bread to form a crispy crust, which also helps fortify the structure of the sandwich, holding it together.

1 tablespoon extra virgin olive oil

1 cup finely diced red onion

1 teaspoon kosher salt

1 large bunch hardy greens (about 12 ounces), washed, stemmed, and chopped

Four 1-inch-thick slices levain or country-style sourdough bread

6 ounces smoked Gouda, sliced

6 ounces aged white cheddar, sliced

2 tablespoons Homemade Mayonnaise (page 14), or store-bought is fine

2 tablespoons butter

Heat the oven to 325ºF.

Place a wide cast-iron skillet over medium heat. When it's hot, add the oil and onions and season with salt. Cook, stirring often, until the onions are translucent and beginning to brown, 3 to 5 minutes. Add a splash of water and then enough greens to fill the pan. Cook, stirring often, until the first batch of greens is wilted down enough to add more. Keep adding the greens and cooking them down until they are all tender and wilted in. You may need to add another splash of water to help steam the greens as they cook down. Continue cooking until most of the moisture has evaporated from the pan and the greens are tender, 6 to 8 minutes. Taste for seasoning and adjust as needed.

Lay the bread slices on a rimmed baking sheet and divide the sliced cheeses evenly among them. Bake until the cheese is just melty, 5 to 6 minutes. Remove the pan from the oven and divide the greens among two of the bread slices, covering the cheese. Place the other two slices on top of the greens, cheese side down, and press the sandwiches together. Spread the mayo across the outside of both the top and bottom of each sandwich. (This will form a crust on the outside when the sandwiches are pan-fried in the skillet.)

Wipe the skillet out to remove any greens residue and return it to medium heat. Melt 1 tablespoon of the butter in the pan, swirling it around to evenly coat the bottom. Place the assembled sandwiches in the skillet and set another skillet (or similar flat, heavy object) on top of them to weigh them down for even cooking. Cook until the bottom sides are nicely browned, then flip each sandwich and repeat, adding the remaining tablespoon of butter and weighing them down again to cook on the second side. Cut the grilled cheese into halves and serve hot.

MUSTARD GREENS AND SPINACH SAAG

Makes 4 servings

On a rather dreary January day while visiting London, we could not shake the bone-chilling, damp cold that was heavy in the air as we walked around the city. Our restaurant list included a posh Indian spot that happened to be nearby, so we dipped inside to escape the cold weather. They served the most elegant version of saag, a blend of mustard greens and spinach with garam masala. Though traditional recipes from the Punjabi region use chickpea flour to thicken the pureed greens, I use unsweetened coconut, which is a nod to the vegetable dishes from the southern region of Kerala.

3 tablespoons ghee

1 small yellow onion, diced

1 serrano chile, minced
(including seeds and ribs)

1 tablespoon minced ginger

1 tablespoon minced garlic

2 teaspoons kosher salt

8 ounces mustard greens, thick
stems trimmed and chopped

8 ounces spinach, chopped

¼ cup desiccated unsweetened
coconut

1 tablespoon Garam Masala
(page 4), or store-bought is fine

Juice of one lemon

In a wide skillet, melt the ghee over medium heat. Add the onions, chile, ginger, garlic, and 1 teaspoon of the salt. Cook, stirring occasionally, until the onions are translucent and the scent is fragrant, about 5 minutes. Add the mustard greens (or as much as will fit in the pan) and cook until wilted down enough to add the spinach. Continue adding the greens by the handful. Once all the greens are added, decrease the heat to medium-low, cover, and cook until they are tender, 12 to 15 minutes. After about 10 minutes, add the coconut, garam masala, and the remaining 1 teaspoon salt.

Transfer the mixture to a food processor and puree until creamy. Add in the lemon juice. Taste for seasoning and adjust to your liking. Before serving, reheat the saag in the skillet over medium-low heat until hot.

SPINACH AND MANCHEGO SOUFFLÉ

Makes 6 servings

If you have never made a soufflé, it is one of those recipes that should be attempted at some point in your cooking journey. There is much mysticism around the technique, but ultimately, it's an easy method to master. In a nutshell, you make a simple béchamel sauce, whip up some egg whites, and fold them both together with whatever flavor will be the accent. Curly Savoy spinach is the inspiration here, because it retains some character and texture after cooking in the oven. Soufflés have a built-in sauce when you pull them from the oven while still a little jiggly. Note that the majestic rise will begin to deflate as soon as it starts to cool, so ring the dinner bell and grab your spoons.

4 tablespoons unsalted butter, plus more for greasing, at room temperature

½ cup chopped yellow onion

2 teaspoons kosher salt

1 pound Savoy spinach leaves

3 tablespoons unbleached all-purpose flour

1 cup whole milk, hot

½ teaspoon dry mustard powder

½ teaspoon paprika

½ teaspoon freshly ground white pepper

¼ teaspoon freshly ground nutmeg

⅛ teaspoon cayenne

5 large eggs at room temperature, yolks and whites separated

1 cup grated Manchego cheese

⅛ teaspoon cream of tartar

Heat the oven to 400°F with a rack in the bottom third and plenty of space above it for the soufflé to rise. Grease the inside of a 1½-quart soufflé dish or straight-sided saucepan with butter and set aside.

In a large skillet, melt 1 tablespoon of the butter over medium heat. Add the onions and 1 teaspoon of the salt and cook, stirring often, until the onions are translucent and beginning to brown, about 5 minutes. Add enough spinach to fill the pan and cook, stirring often, until it has wilted down enough to add more. Keep adding the spinach a handful at a time and cook until it's all tender and wilted. Turn off the heat and transfer the spinach to a fine-mesh sieve. Holding the sieve over the skillet, squeeze out as much liquid from the spinach as you can. Transfer the squeezed spinach to a cutting board and coarsely chop it.

Return the pan of spinach juice to medium heat and simmer until it is reduced to about 2 tablespoons. Remove the pan from the heat and add the chopped spinach back in, tossing to coat it in the reduced juice; set aside.

In a medium saucepan, melt the remaining 3 tablespoons of butter over medium heat. Whisk in the flour and cook, whisking constantly, for 2 minutes. Slowly pour in the hot milk while continuing to whisk until the mixture becomes smooth. Add the remaining 1 teaspoon salt, the dry mustard, paprika, white pepper, nutmeg, and cayenne and cook over low heat until thick and smooth, about 1 minute. Remove the pan from the heat and whisk in the egg yolks one at a time. Add the spinach mixture and the grated cheese and stir well to combine; set aside.

Place the egg whites and cream of tartar in the bowl of an electric mixer and turn the motor on low speed. Slowly increase the speed to high and beat until the mixture forms firm, glossy peaks.

Gently whisk about one-third of the egg whites into the spinach mixture. Then, using a spatula, carefully fold in the remaining whites in two batches. Transfer the soufflé batter to the prepared dish, and using the tip of the spatula, make a shallow circular indentation in the center of the top of the batter.

Immediately place the soufflé in the oven and bake until the soufflé is mostly set but still a little jiggly in the center when nudged, 30 to 35 minutes. Be sure not to open the oven door too early; it is safer to peek closer to the end of the cooking time, when the top of the soufflé has set. When finished, the soufflé will be a deep golden brown across the top, with some cracks and ripples exposing the tender egg mixture inside. Serve immediately, using two spoons to pull up from the center when portioning, so that each serving has a little from the middle and a little from the outer edge.

PORTUGUESE BREAD SOUP WITH CHARD AND CILANTRO

Makes 4 to 6 servings

I think of this as a friendship soup, the kind of recipe that gets passed around and shared. I first learned of it when I read an article written by Scott Hocker about this humble dish that reawakens stale bread in a flavorful, cilantro-laced broth with greens and poached eggs. His version was an adaptation from Bar Tartine in San Francisco, which was in his neighborhood. And now I offer my version to you, my friends. This is a memorable dish that you will want to share with others and keep passing along.

1 bunch cilantro, chopped (including stems)

1 clove garlic, minced

½ cup extra virgin olive oil

1 bunch Swiss chard

1 cup diced white onion

1 tablespoon kosher salt, plus a pinch

6 cups Roasted Chicken Stock (page 11), or store-bought is fine

1½ cups cooked white beans (canned are okay), such as cannellini, flageolet, or navy beans, drained

1 tablespoon fresh lemon juice

½ teaspoon freshly ground black pepper, plus more to garnish

1 tablespoon distilled vinegar

4 to 6 large eggs

1 recipe Garlic Croutons (page 25)

Place the cilantro, garlic, and ¼ cup of the oil in a food processor and process until well combined. Scrape the mixture into a bowl and set aside.

Wash the chard and pat dry. Remove the leaves from the stems and tear them into large pieces. Dice the stems and keep them separate.

In a 6-quart Dutch oven, heat the remaining ¼ cup oil over medium heat. Add the onions and chard stems and season with 2 teaspoons of the salt. Cook until the onions are translucent and the chard stems are tender, 5 to 6 minutes. Add the chicken stock and bring to a simmer. Add the drained beans and the chard leaves and simmer until the chard is tender, 10 to 15 minutes. Add the lemon juice and season with the remaining 1 teaspoon salt and the black pepper. Taste for seasoning and adjust to your liking. Turn the heat down as low as possible and place a lid on top of the soup to keep it warm until you're ready to serve.

Meanwhile, in a separate, small saucepan, heat 3 cups of water with the vinegar and a pinch of salt. When it reaches a simmer, swirl the water with a spoon and crack one of the eggs into the center. Repeat the swirling process for each additional egg until they are all in the water. Cook gently until they are soft poached, about 3 minutes. Remove the eggs from the poaching liquid using a slotted spoon and set them on a plate lined with paper towels to absorb any excess water.

Divide the croutons among serving bowls, and ladle in the soup. Add a poached egg to each bowl and finish with the cilantro sauce and more black pepper.

BABY KALE AND STRAWBERRY SALAD

Makes 4 main-course servings, or 6 to 8 as a side dish

Most kale salads benefit from either finely chopping the kale or massaging the dressing into the mature leaves to soften them. But when kale is in the young, tender stage, as in this recipe, it's a different story. A zippy strawberry vinaigrette coats the leaves, while more sliced berries and fresh chèvre are mixed with the earthy greens. I usually serve this salad in the springtime, when the new vintage of rosé wines is released.

8 ounces young, tender kale leaves

1 pint strawberries

½ cup chopped green garlic, white and green parts (see Note)

¼ cup white balsamic vinegar

1 teaspoon whole-grain mustard

1 teaspoon kosher salt

¼ teaspoon freshly ground black pepper

¼ cup extra virgin olive oil

1 cup sliced celery hearts

4 ounces chèvre cheese, crumbled

½ cup roasted pecan halves (see page 24)

Depending on the maturity of the baby kale you find (toddler or teenager), there may be some tough, fibrous stems. If so, remove the stems from each kale leaf by lightly pinching the leaf together and pulling the stem upward. (The stems can be saved for juicing or used in the Portuguese Bread Soup with Chard and Cilantro on page 97.)

Fill a large bowl or your clean kitchen sink with water and submerge the kale leaves. Pull the leaves out and place in a salad spinner, leaving the water, and any dirt that sinks to the bottom, behind. Spin or pat the kale dry and set aside.

Drop the strawberries into the water ever so briefly and pull them out immediately. (You don't want strawberries to sit in water for any length of time as they are porous and will absorb water almost instantly.) Drain and pat dry. Remove the green tops with a paring knife and cut the strawberries into halves if small or quarters if large.

In a blender, combine ¼ cup of the strawberries, the green garlic, vinegar, mustard, salt, and pepper. Blend on high until it's a smooth puree. With the motor running, drizzle in the oil to emulsify. Taste for seasoning and adjust to your liking.

In a large bowl, toss the kale and celery with enough of the dressing to lightly coat. Divide the salad among plates and top with the strawberries, chèvre, and pecans.

NOTE: If green garlic is unavailable, substitute an equal amount of chopped green onions plus 1 clove of garlic, minced.

KALE FRENCH TOAST

Makes 4 servings

Inspired by a dish I enjoyed at a trattoria in Siena, Italy, this savory take on French toast blends kale and eggs into a vibrant green batter for stale bread to soak up. I've served this with a number of different toppings, like smoked salmon, roasted vegetables, and soft-ripened cheese with fruit jam. Or give it a breakfast moment with fried ham and a sunny egg.

5 ounces lacinato kale, coarsely chopped (including stems)

2 large eggs

1/2 teaspoon kosher salt

Four 1-inch-thick slices stale country sourdough bread

4 tablespoons unsalted butter

Place the kale in a blender with 3/4 cup water and blend on high until it is as smooth as possible. Add the eggs and salt and blend again until smooth. Pour the mixture into a wide, shallow baking dish that will fit all the bread slices snugly in a single layer. Add the bread slices, turning to coat each one on all sides in the sauce. Set aside for the bread to absorb the kale mixture, 10 to 15 minutes.

Heat the oven to 200°F. Set a wire rack in a rimmed baking sheet and place it near the stove.

Place a large nonstick or cast iron skillet over medium-high heat. Add 1 tablespoon of the butter and swirl it around to evenly coat the bottom of the pan. Add two slices of the soaked bread and reduce the heat to medium. Cook until the undersides are a little crisp and browned, 3 to 4 minutes. Flip, adding another tablespoon of butter to the edges of the pan. Cook on the second side for 3 to 4 minutes more. Transfer the cooked French toast to the wire rack and place it in the oven to keep warm while you cook the remaining batch in the same way.

Serve the French toast with the toppings of your choice.

ARUGULA "DRAG" SALAD

Makes 4 to 6 servings

I'm not talking about RuPaul here. When I serve a thick dressing with a salad, I prefer to spread it across the bottom of the plate so as not to weigh down the tender leaves. The salad is piled on top of the schmear, and pulled through the creaminess underneath, so that each bite is perfectly coated. I call this all-in-one motion "the salad drag."

5 ounces arugula

1 small fennel bulb

1 small, thin-skinned cucumber, such as Kirby, English, or Persian

2 plums

1 recipe Honeyed Lemon Yogurt (page 15)

1 tablespoon extra virgin olive oil

1 teaspoon fresh lemon juice

1/2 teaspoon kosher salt

1/2 teaspoon fennel pollen (optional)

Torn squash blossoms or edible flowers (optional)

Wash the arugula if it comes in bunches, or if it needs to be refreshed from a prewashed package, then dry in a salad spinner.

Very thinly slice the fennel bulb crosswise, either with a mandoline or by hand with a sharp chef's knife. Slice the cucumber crosswise in the same way. Halve the plums, remove the pits, and slice them into wedges.

Spread the yogurt onto individual plates, dividing it evenly. In a large bowl, gently toss the arugula, fennel, cucumber, and plums with the oil, lemon juice, and salt. Pile the salad on top of the yogurt on each plate. Sprinkle the salads with fennel pollen and flower petals, if you have some handy.

CHICKEN SCHNITZEL WITH CREAMED WATERCRESS

Makes 4 servings

I have an affinity for peppery greens and my favorite is watercress. This delicate green can be high on the spicy spectrum, so it often needs tempering with a little salt and fat, much like you would treat a spicy radish. When it is cooked, it has a deep minerality, like robust spinach, and it can handle the richness of a little heavy cream. I can't think of a better pairing alongside a crispy pan-fried chicken cutlet, but if you cannot find watercress, arugula or spinach will be a fine understudy.

Two 8- to 10-ounce boneless, skinless chicken breasts, patted dry

2¼ teaspoons fine sea salt

1 teaspoon freshly ground black pepper

1 cup buttermilk

2 cups fine white bread crumbs

Canola oil, for frying

1 recipe Creamed Watercress (recipe follows)

4 ounces watercress, thick stems trimmed

1 lemon

Line a cutting board with plastic film and secure the board underneath with a damp towel or a rubber grip so it won't slip. Place one chicken breast on top of the plastic and cover it with another sheet of plastic film. Using the smooth side of a meat mallet, pound the breast out until it is about ½-inch thick. Repeat with the second breast, starting with fresh plastic film if the first two tear from the pounding. Cut each flattened breast in half crosswise. Season the chicken pieces on all sides with 1¼ teaspoons of the salt and ½ teaspoon of the pepper, coating them evenly, and let sit while you make the creamed watercress (recipe follows).

Pour the buttermilk into a casserole dish or straight-sided baking pan. Place the bread crumbs in a separate dish or baking pan and season them with the remaining 1 teaspoon of salt and remaining ½ teaspoon black pepper. Using one hand and keeping the other dry, lay the chicken pieces in the buttermilk, coating both sides. Pick up the chicken pieces with your wet hand and lay them in the bread crumbs. Using the dry hand, sprinkle the bread crumbs across the wet surface of the chicken and press to adhere. Flip and repeat to thoroughly coat all sides.

Fill a cast-iron skillet or other wide, heavy frying pan with enough oil to come about 1 to 1½ inches up the side of the pan and place it over medium heat. Position a thermometer in the oil, and begin frying when it reaches 350°F. Gently lower two of the breaded pieces of chicken into the pan, or enough to fit in a single layer without overlapping. (Be careful not to overcrowd the pan.) Fry on each side until the bread crumbs become golden brown and crispy, 3 to 4 minutes per side. Adjust the heat as needed to maintain the oil temperature throughout frying. Use a slotted spoon or spatula to remove the fried chicken breasts from the pan as they are done and transfer them to a platter lined with paper towels. Repeat to fry the remaining chicken.

Spoon the creamed watercress onto 4 plates and place the schnitzel on top. Add the raw watercress in a loose pile next to the chicken, dividing it evenly, and squeeze half of the lemon over everything. Cut the remaining half of the lemon into wedges and place one on each plate.

Continue to next page for Creamed Watercress

CREAMED WATERCRESS

Makes 4 servings

8 ounces watercress, or other peppery greens such as arugula, mizuna, or mustard greens

2 tablespoons unsalted butter

1 cup diced yellow onion

1 tablespoon chopped garlic

1/2 teaspoon fine sea salt

1/4 teaspoon freshly ground black pepper

1/2 cup heavy cream

CREAMED WATERCRESS: Trim the thick stems from the watercress and coarsely chop the leaves and thinner stems.

In a medium skillet, melt the butter over medium-high heat. Add the onions, garlic, salt, and pepper and cook, stirring often, until the onions are translucent and beginning to brown, 4 to 5 minutes. Stir in the cream and scrape up any bits stuck to the bottom of the pan. Add as much of the chopped greens as will fit in the pan and cook until they wilt down enough to add more. Continue adding the greens by the handful until they are all in. Cook until the cream sauce thickens a bit and the greens are tender, 5 to 8 minutes. Taste for seasoning and adjust to your liking.

DANDELION PAPPARDELLE
Makes 4 servings

Dandelion is a harbinger of early spring. You often see clusters of the leaves popping up in grassy areas or even cracks in the sidewalk. Although a common sight, it's better to buy them from a farmer, as the ones you stumble upon could be a target for the neighborhood doggie stroll. In this recipe, the dandelion leaves are sautéed until just tender, then pulverized with eggs and flour to make a verdant pasta dough. The stems are reserved for textural contrast and cooked alongside spring alliums or a light creamy sauce.

1 bunch dandelion greens (about 6 ounces)

2 tablespoons extra virgin olive oil

2 large eggs, plus 1 large egg yolk

2½ cups all-purpose flour, plus more for dusting

2 bulby spring onions or 1 bunch green onions, white and green parts thinly sliced

3 tablespoons kosher salt, plus more to taste

4 ounces mascarpone cheese

Herbs or flowers to garnish

Place the dandelion greens on a cutting board and trim the bottom ½ inch of the stems. Cut the bottom third of the bunch, separating the leggy stems from the green tops. Wash the tops and bottoms separately and dry them in a salad spinner. Coarsely chop the leaves and slice the stems crosswise into ½-inch pieces, and set them aside in separate bowls.

In a medium skillet, heat 1 tablespoon of the oil over medium heat. Add the chopped dandelion leaves and cook until wilted and tender, about 2 minutes. Transfer the greens to a blender or food processor and blitz until they are as finely minced as possible. Add the whole eggs and yolk and process until well combined, scraping down the sides as needed. There will be some texture to the mixture, which gives the pasta character.

Place the flour in a medium bowl and make a well in the center. Pour the greens-and-egg mixture into the well. Using a fork, whisk in the center of the well, slowly incorporating the flour into the wet mixture until most of the flour is moistened and a shaggy dough forms. Transfer the dough to a floured surface and knead by pressing the heel of your hand into the dough and pushing away from you on the work surface, turning and repeating, until a firm ball forms that resembles the texture of Play-Doh. If the dough feels too wet, simply sprinkle it and the work surface with a little more flour and work it in. Flatten the ball into a thick disk and wrap it tightly in plastic film, then refrigerate for at least 1 hour and up to 1 day before rolling it out.

To roll the pasta dough, remove it from the refrigerator and let sit at room temperature for 20 minutes. Place some flour in a small bowl for dusting. Cut the disk into 4 pieces and cover three of them with plastic film until ready to use. Flatten out the remaining piece with the palm of your hand and shape it into an oval that is thin enough to fit in the widest setting of your pasta roller. Lightly flour your work surface and the piece of dough and pass the dough again through the roller. (It's okay if the dough tears; just refold and continue to run through until the dough achieves enough elasticity to be resilient.) Lay out the rolled sheet of pasta and lightly dust it with more flour, brushing away any excess. Fold the dough over in thirds, turn it 90 degrees, and pass it through the roller once again through the widest setting. Repeat dusting with flour, brushing away any excess with your

Continue to page 109 for the rest of the recipe

fingers, and passing again through the roller, each time with the progressively narrower setting, until the dough is ⅛-inch thick. Using a pasta cutter or sharp knife, cut the dough into 1-inch-wide strips. Transfer the noodles to a rimmed baking sheet generously dusted with flour. Repeat until all the pasta is rolled and cut. Set the noodles aside at room temperature for up to 2 hours or wrap the baking sheet tightly with plastic film and refrigerate for up to 1 day.

Bring 4 quarts of water to a boil in a large pot over high heat and add the 3 tablespoons salt.

Meanwhile, in a wide sauté pan, warm the remaining 1 tablespoon oil over medium-low heat until it shimmers. Add the onions and dandelion stems and season lightly with salt. Sauté until the stems and onions are tenderized, 2 to 3 minutes. Stir in the mascarpone until it is fully incorporated and creamy, then remove the pan from the heat and set aside while you cook the pasta.

Once the water has reached a full boil, drop the noodles into the water and stir them immediately to prevent them from sticking together. Cook until the noodles are tender but still a little chewy to the bite, about 2 minutes. Immediately pull the noodles from the water with tongs or a slotted spoon and place them in a colander to drain, reserving some of the pasta water for finishing the dish.

Return the pan of sauce to medium-high heat and add the cooked noodles. Add a few tablespoons of the pasta water to revive the sauce. Toss or stir gently until the pasta is coated well and taste for seasoning. Adjust the seasoning as desired and serve immediately.

ESCAROLE AND SARDINE SALAD

Makes 4 to 6 servings

Escarole is one of those greens that is underutilized but has amazing versatility. I love it sautéed with onion, garlic, and olive oil and wilted into a soup or stew. In fact, it is the green featured in the famous Italian wedding soup. The outer, darker leaves tend to show more bitterness, while the interior leaves have a sweeter, milder flavor. When served raw, its juicy crunch pairs perfectly with bold flavors. Use it to make an impromptu entrée salad for those of us who always have a tin of fancy sardines on hand. Don't skimp on the garlic bread crumbs; they add a satisfying crunch, which you'll thank me for later.

1 large head escarole
(about 1 pound)

1 bunch radishes

2 (4-ounce) tins Mediterranean
sardines packed in olive oil

1 recipe French Vinaigrette
(page 18)

1 cup Toasted Garlic Bread Crumbs
(page 25)

Place the escarole on a cutting board, trim the root end, and remove any weathered or discolored outer leaves. Cut the head of escarole in half through the root end, then lay each half on the cutting board and slice them into large bite-size pieces. Fill a large bowl or your clean kitchen sink with water and submerge the escarole leaves. Pull the leaves out and place them in a salad spinner, leaving the water, and any dirt that sinks to the bottom, behind. Spin the escarole dry.

Trim the tops of the radishes. If the tops look fresh and healthy, you can wash and spin them dry and add them to the escarole or save them for another use. Wash the radishes and cut them into quarters, or smaller wedges if they are large.

Open the tin of sardines and drain them. Using a fork, flake the sardines into bite-size pieces.

Toss the escarole with enough of the vinaigrette to nicely coat. Taste for seasoning and adjust to your liking. Divide the salad among 4 plates. Add the radishes then the sardines to each salad and top with bread crumbs.

BELGIAN ENDIVE PINTXOS

Makes 24 to 30 pintxos

I was lucky enough to spend a week in San Sebastian several years ago with a group of friends. We spent days combing the beach and hiking the nearby hills, and nights barhopping and tasting all the pintxos. Spain's Basque Country has a fun tradition of turning dinner into a roving bar crawl, with different bite-size snacks served at each stop. Belgian endive is the perfect vessel for a tasty handheld pintxo, and these were created in the spirit of this style of eating. Toss a few back with a chilled bottle of txakolina, the region's sparkling wine, or some dry sherry. Salud!

8 ounces creamy blue cheese, like Valdeon, St. Agur, or Gorgonzola Dolce

3 heads Belgian endive

3/4 cup coarsely chopped Medjool dates

3/4 cup pickled hot banana peppers, sliced into rings

3 slices Crispy Cured Ham (page 25), broken into small pieces

1/4 cup flat-leaf parsley leaves

Extra virgin olive oil, to finish

Place the blue cheese in a bowl and mash with a fork or the back of a spoon into a spreadable consistency.

Place the endive on a cutting board and trim the base from each head. Pull apart individual leaves and line them up on the cutting board; you should be able to get between 24 and 30 leaves that are large enough to stuff. (Reserve the remaining smaller leaves for a salad.)

Assemble the pintxos by spreading the blue cheese into the endive leaves, dividing it evenly. Top the cheese with a few pieces of the dates, pickled pepper rings, and crispy ham. Garnish with the parsley leaves and drizzle with the olive oil.

RADICCHIO SALAD WITH BAGNA CAUDA VINAIGRETTE

Makes 6 servings

Autumn is the time for chicories, and radicchio is my favorite of them all. The most commonly recognized radicchio variety is the round chioggia, which looks like a small maroon-and-white cabbage. There are many other varieties, from the elongated, pale-green sugarloaf to the chartreuse-and-pink-speckled Castelfranco and the romaine-like crimson Treviso. Whichever varieties you stumble upon, grab them all and make this salad. The garlicky, anchovy-laden dressing is inspired by Italian bagna cauda, which means "warm bath," but in this case it's a cold vinaigrette. Persimmons add contrasting sweetness, while oil-cured olives bring intense umami to the mix.

1 small head radicchio
(8 to 12 ounces)

1 ripe Fuyu persimmon

About ½ cup Bagna Cauda
Vinaigrette (page 20)

¼ cup oil-cured black olives,
pitted and torn

Trim the base of the radicchio and cut it into quarters through the core. Trim the core from each quarter and separate the leaves. Fill a large bowl or your clean kitchen sink with water and submerge the leaves. Pull the leaves from the water, leaving the water, and any dirt that sinks to the bottom, behind. Spin in a salad spinner or pat with a kitchen towel to dry.

Place the persimmon on a cutting board, peel the skin, and remove the leaves. Halve the persimmon and cut it into thin, half-moon slices, removing any seeds.

Arrange the radicchio in a large bowl and toss with enough of the vinaigrette to lightly coat. Transfer the salad to a serving platter. Add the persimmon slices and the olives and drizzle a little more of the dressing on top.

STALKS

Assembled here is a band of misfit vegetables that share one common trait: they all grow as stalks. For cooking purposes, I tend to classify stalks based on their structure or texture.

Rhubarb and asparagus emerge in the spring and behave in a similar way when cooked but have vastly different flavors and uses. They each have a fibrous skin surrounding a crisp interior flesh that quickly tenderizes to a supple texture when cooked. There's a critical point when grilled asparagus and roasted rhubarb are perfectly al dente in the middle. Cooked longer, they turn to mush, which is a desired effect for making rhubarb jam or asparagus soup.

Then there are the clustered stalks, like celery and fennel. Both are fibrous and crunchy when raw, and ideal for thinly slicing into a refreshing salad or turning into a creamy slaw. Their flavor becomes mellow and sweet, and their texture is rendered meltingly soft when slow-cooked in the oven or on the stove. At the top of these stalks are leaves; celery leaves have an herbal flavor akin to parsley, and fennel fronds have an anise note. Use them as you would fresh herbs. And though the fennel is prized for its bulb, note the stalks are edible, versatile, and just as delicious.

Corn, okra, and artichokes all come from the flowering, edible part of their stalks. Sweet corn is the epitome of summer, whether it is grilled on the cob with a spicy twist, or cut off, creamed, and loaded with herbs. Okra, a Southern staple, loves the heat of summer, and is a crisp-tender pod when grilled. It also makes a unique thickening agent when braised or stewed. Perhaps no other vegetable is as meaty as the artichoke after it is steamed, grilled, or roasted. A flower in the thistle family, the artichoke has a protective coat of armor surrounding its edible base. To expose the heart of the choke, the thick petals must be carved away. However, if you are steaming an artichoke whole, the interior side of the outer leaves is edible too.

FENNEL GRATIN

Makes 6 to 8 servings

When fennel is cooked long and slow, it develops a mellow sweetness and meltingly soft texture. In this mac-and-cheese-inspired gratin, strands of sliced fennel are baked in a creamy béchamel sauce with nutty gruyère and sharp white cheddar. It may very well become your new favorite indulgence, and the bonus is there are vegetables in every forkful.

4 large or 6 small fennel bulbs

5 tablespoons unsalted butter

5 tablespoons all-purpose flour

3½ cups whole milk, warmed

5 ounces gruyère cheese, grated (about 2 cups)

5 ounces aged white cheddar cheese, grated (about 2 cups)

1 tablespoon kosher salt

½ teaspoon freshly ground black pepper

1 cup plain dry bread crumbs

Heat the oven to 375°F with a rack in the center.

Cut the fennel bulb into ⅛-inch-thick matchsticks following the instructions on page 73. Place the fennel in a shallow, 2-quart baking dish and set aside.

In a medium saucepan, melt the butter over medium heat. Add the flour and cook, stirring constantly, for 2 minutes. Slowly whisk in the warm milk until smooth. Bring to a gentle simmer and cook for 2 minutes. Add both cheeses and the salt and pepper, and whisk until the cheese is melted and incorporated.

Pour the cheese sauce over the fennel and stir well to combine. Scatter the bread crumbs evenly across the surface of the fennel and press them with the palms of your hands so that they get coated in some of the cheese sauce.

Place the dish on a rimmed baking sheet and bake, uncovered, until the crumbs on top are deep golden brown and the cheese sauce is hot and bubbling, about 1 hour. Let cool for 10 to 15 minutes before serving.

CELERY SALAD WITH PEAR, PUMPKIN SEEDS, AND BLUE CHEESE

Makes 6 to 8 servings

Nothing beats the satisfying crunch of a celery salad. It's crisp, light, refreshing, and healthy. Here I accent the crisp stalks with really good blue cheese, sliced pears, and toasted pumpkin seeds, but you can use any cheese, fall fruit, nut, or seed on hand. Banyuls vinegar, which is made from a sweet wine in southwestern France, brings a complex flavor to the salad, but sherry vinegar and a touch more honey will do.

¼ cup Banyuls vinegar

2 tablespoons extra virgin olive oil

1 tablespoon honey

2 teaspoons kosher salt

½ teaspoon piment d'Espelette (see Note), plus more for garnish

1 head celery

1 ripe Bartlett or Anjou pear, quartered lengthwise, cored, and thinly sliced crosswise

1 cup toasted pumpkin seeds (see page 24)

4 ounces firm blue cheese, such as Stilton, Rogue River, or Roquefort

Flaky sea salt

In a large bowl, whisk the vinegar, oil, honey, kosher salt, and piment d'Espelette and set aside.

Place the head of celery on a cutting board and remove the base. Trim any weathered tips at the top of the head and remove any leaves or stalks that don't look fresh (but do save the castoffs to make stock). Wash the celery ribs under cold water, running your finger down the center of each stalk to check for dirt or sand that may be clinging.

Arrange the stalks two at a time on the cutting board and thinly slice them crosswise on a slight bias, including the leaves. Transfer the sliced celery to the bowl of dressing and add the pear slices and pumpkin seeds. Toss the salad together and transfer it to a serving platter or bowl. Crumble the blue cheese on top and sprinkle with flaky sea salt and a little more of the piment d'Espelette.

NOTE: Piment d'Espelette is a fragrant, mildly spicy chile powder that hails from the town of Espelette in the Basque region of France. It can be found at specialty food stores, spice shops, or online. A suitable alternative is hot paprika.

CREAMY FENNEL SLAW

Makes 4 to 6 servings

Fennel bulbs can be shaved on a mandoline or sliced with a knife in a matter of minutes for a fresh slaw. What many don't realize is that you can use fennel stalks too. I usually serve this alongside a simple plate of beans, rice, and avocado, though it is also great as a component of a larger meal. Keep it in your back pocket for a quick, crunchy fix.

1 large fennel bulb (about 1 pound)

About ½ recipe Lime-Pickled Red Onions (page 30)

1 teaspoon finely grated lime zest

½ teaspoon ground coriander

½ teaspoon ground cumin

½ teaspoon fine sea salt

¼ cup sour cream

Trim and discard the root end of the fennel bulb. Remove the stalks from the bulb and thinly slice them crosswise into coins, reserving the fronds for another use. Cut the bulb in half lengthwise and use the tip of the knife to make a triangular cut to remove most of the core from each half. Slice the bulb very thinly, either using a mandoline or by placing the cut sides down on the cutting board and using a sharp chef's knife.

Place the fennel, pickled onions, and about 1 tablespoon of the pickling juice in a medium bowl and toss with the lime zest, coriander, cumin, and salt. Mix well to combine, then add the sour cream and stir until everything is evenly distributed. Taste for seasoning and adjust to your liking. If you'd like it a little more tart, add another splash of the pickling juice. Serve immediately or within a couple of hours.

HOMEMADE CELERY SODA

Makes enough for 6 drinks

Kids and adults alike will get a kick out of these homemade refreshing drinks. They each start with a simple syrup infused with celery or rhubarb and can be batched ahead of time for serving at your leisure. The celery soda is my take on the nostalgic Dr. Brown's Cel-Ray, which has been popular in Jewish delis and health-food stores for decades. And this rhubarb lemonade is what pink lemonade should be: tart, sweet, and made from natural ingredients instead of artificial flavorings. Of course, if you want to turn these into adult beverages, just stir in your favorite clear distilled spirit.

1 pound celery stalks, including leaves, trimmed and chopped

3/4 cup granulated sugar

2 teaspoons celery seeds

1 cup fresh lime juice

1/2 teaspoon fine sea salt

Club soda

In a medium saucepan, combine the celery, sugar, celery seeds, and 1½ cups of water and bring to a lively simmer over medium-high heat. Stir briefly just to dissolve the sugar. Adjust the heat to maintain a gentle simmer and cook, undisturbed, until the celery is very soft, about 20 minutes. Remove from the heat and set aside to cool completely.

Strain the celery mixture through a sieve into a container. Avoid pressing down on the solids to have a nice clear syrup. Stir in the lime juice and salt and refrigerate the celery syrup until ready to use, or for up to 1 week.

To make each drink, pour 3 ounces of the syrup into a glass filled with ice and top with 6 ounces of club soda.

FOR A SPIKED VERSION: Pour 3 ounces of the syrup and 1½ ounces of vodka (or the clear spirit of your choice) into a glass filled with ice and top with 4 ounces of club soda.

RHUBARB LEMONADE

Makes enough for 6 drinks

1 pound rhubarb, trimmed and chopped

3/4 cup granulated sugar

1 cup fresh lemon juice

1/2 teaspoon fine sea salt

Club soda

In a medium saucepan, combine the rhubarb, sugar, and 1½ cups of water and bring to a lively simmer over medium-high heat. Stir briefly just to dissolve the sugar. Adjust the heat to maintain a gentle simmer and cook, undisturbed, until the rhubarb is very soft, about 20 minutes. Remove from the heat and set aside to cool completely.

Strain the rhubarb mixture through a sieve into a container. Avoid pressing down on the solids to have a nice clear syrup. Stir in the lemon juice and salt and refrigerate the rhubarb syrup until ready to use, or for up to 1 week.

To make each drink, pour 3 ounces of the rhubarb syrup into a glass filled with ice and top with 6 ounces of club soda.

FOR A SPIKED VERSION: Pour 3 ounces of the syrup and 1½ ounces of vodka (or the clear spirit of your choice) into a glass filled with ice and top with 4 ounces of club soda.

RHUBARB-ALMOND CREAM PIE

Makes one 9-inch, deep-dish pie

I am no pastry chef, so when I construct a dessert, I try to make it as uncomplicated as possible. There are three main components to this pie: a simple cookie crust that is very forgiving; a whipped, light-as-air cream filling; and thick-sliced rhubarb that is lightly roasted with honey and orange. The filling is layered with some roasted almonds for added crunch and piled with the bright pink rhubarb. Each time I've made this cream pie, it's been devoured in a matter of minutes.

CRUST

1½ cups all-purpose flour

¼ cup almond flour

½ teaspoon kosher salt

6 tablespoons (¾ stick) unsalted butter, softened

½ cup powdered sugar

1 egg, at room temperature

RHUBARB TOPPING

1¼ pounds rhubarb, trimmed and cut into ¾-inch pieces

Juice of 1 navel orange

6 tablespoons honey

¼ teaspoon kosher salt

TO MAKE THE CRUST: In a large bowl, combine the all-purpose flour, almond flour, and salt and set aside. In a stand mixer fitted with the paddle attachment, or in a large mixing bowl using a handheld electric mixer, cream the butter on low speed until smooth. Turn off the mixer, scrape down the sides of the bowl, and add the powdered sugar. Mix on low until smooth and creamy, about 1 minute. Add the egg and continue to mix until well combined, about 1 minute, stopping to scrape the sides of the bowl as needed. Stop the mixer and add about one-third of the flour mixture. Mix until the flour is incorporated, then add the remaining flour in two more batches and mix until the dough just comes together. Tip the dough out onto a piece of plastic film, and bring it together to form a ball. Flatten the ball into a disk and wrap it tightly in the plastic. Chill the dough for at least 2 hours or overnight.

Let the chilled dough sit at room temperature for a few minutes to soften slightly, or for about 30 minutes if it was chilled overnight. Using a rolling pin, roll out the dough between 2 sheets of parchment paper until it is about 14 inches in diameter. Remove the top sheet of parchment and swiftly invert the crust into a 9-inch deep-dish pie plate. If it crumbles or tears, that is okay; this dough is very forgiving and you can simply press it into the dish with your fingers, patching up any holes. Be sure to press the dough into the corner of the dish and up the sides evenly. Using scissors, trim the excess dough hanging over the edges. Prick the dough with the tines of a fork then refrigerate until well chilled, 20 to 30 minutes.

Heat the oven to 350°F. Remove the chilled dough and cover it with a new sheet of parchment paper. Place enough pie weights or dried beans on the parchment to cover the bottom in an even layer and bake for 20 minutes. Remove the weights and parchment and return the crust to the oven to continue baking until it is golden and crisp but not too deeply browned, 5 to 10 minutes more. Set aside to cool completely.

TO MAKE THE TOPPING: In a medium bowl, combine the rhubarb with the orange juice, honey, and salt. Mix well then transfer the mixture to a large rimmed baking sheet and roast until the rhubarb is tender but still holds its shape, 8 to 12 minutes. Set aside to cool completely.

Continue to next page for Cream Filling

CREAM FILLING

8 ounces mascarpone cheese

1 cup heavy cream

3/4 cup powdered sugar

1 teaspoon pure vanilla extract

Zest of 1 navel orange

1/4 teaspoon kosher salt

1 cup roasted sliced almonds
(see page 24)

TO MAKE THE FILLING: In a stand mixer fitted with the whisk attachment, or in a large mixing bowl using a handheld electric mixer, combine the mascarpone, cream, powdered sugar, vanilla, orange zest, and salt. Beat on medium speed until it's light and airy and will hold peaks, 6 to 7 minutes. Cover and refrigerate until ready to use.

TO ASSEMBLE THE PIE: Spread half of the cream mixture in the bottom of the pie crust. Sprinkle half of the almonds on top of the cream, then spread the remaining cream on top of the almonds. Sprinkle the second layer of cream with the remaining almonds. Spoon the roasted rhubarb over the top. The pie can be served immediately or chilled overnight.

ASPARAGUS BOTTOM SOUP

Makes 4 servings

During asparagus season, save the bottoms of your asparagus bunches to make this quick and resourceful soup. Of course, you could make this soup with tender asparagus stalks too, but it's a great way to avoid wasting any of this prized spring vegetable. You could apply this same method to broccoli stalks too.

8 ounces asparagus bottoms

1 cup thinly sliced kale stems, leaves, or a mix of both

2 tablespoons unsalted butter

2 tablespoons extra virgin olive oil

1 small yellow onion, coarsely chopped

2 cloves garlic, chopped, or 1 stalk green garlic, sliced

¼ teaspoon crushed red pepper

2½ teaspoons kosher salt, plus more to taste

4 cups Seasonal Vegetable Stock or Roasted Chicken Stock (page 11), or store-bought, water, or a combination is fine

1 bunch chives, thinly sliced

Garlic Croutons or Toasted Garlic Bread Crumbs (page 25), or Crispy Cured Ham (page 25) for garnish

Place the asparagus bottoms on a cutting board and trim away any crusty or brown parts. Slice them crosswise into thin pieces. Slice the kale stems and/or leaves and set aside.

In a medium Dutch oven, heat the butter and olive oil over medium heat. When the butter is melted, add the onions, garlic, crushed red pepper, and salt. Cook, stirring often, until the onions are translucent, about 5 minutes. Add the asparagus and kale and cook, stirring often, until the asparagus is aromatic and just tender, about 5 minutes more. Add the stock and/or water and bring to a simmer. Adjust the heat to maintain a gentle simmer and cook until the asparagus and kale are very tender and the flavors meld, 12 to 15 minutes.

Puree the soup in a blender in two batches until velvety smooth, 2 to 3 minutes per batch. Because you're working with the fibrous parts of the vegetables, it's important to blend the soup long enough to break them down. Taste for seasoning and adjust to your liking.

Ladle the soup into warm bowls and garnish with chives and the crunchy topping of your choice.

GRILLED ASPARAGUS AND SAFFRON AIOLI

Makes 4 servings

One of my earliest memories of eating asparagus was in the late '80s when I was working as a server at a high-end hotel while finishing college. The French chef grilled thick stalks of asparagus and served them with a saffron aioli. The flavor combination made an impact, and I still remember the taste today. I appreciate asparagus of all sizes, but jumbo is my favorite because it has a more meaty, juicy texture. Be sure to make the aioli first so that the saffron threads have time to permeate the emulsion, infusing it with vivid yellow color and distinct flavor. This is a great recipe for using a grill pan if you don't already have the grill fired up.

1 pound large or jumbo asparagus

2 teaspoons olive oil

1 teaspoon kosher salt

½ teaspoon freshly ground black pepper

2 tablespoons fresh tarragon leaves

1 recipe Saffron Aioli (page 14)

Heat the grill. If using gas, set to medium-high. If cooking over wood or charcoal, allow the flames to die down until the embers are glowing. If using a grill pan, place it over medium-high heat just before cooking.

Line up the asparagus spears on a cutting board and trim off the bottom 2 inches, or wherever they begin to get tough and woody. (The bottoms can be reserved to make Asparagus Bottom Soup on page 129.) Wash them well and pat dry. Place the asparagus in a shallow dish, rub them with the oil, and sprinkle with the salt and pepper.

Place the asparagus on the grill, arranging them perpendicular to the grates so they don't fall through. (If you're using a grill pan, cook in batches and place a heavy skillet on top of the asparagus to weigh them down while cooking.) Cook, turning occasionally, until nicely charred on all sides, 5 to 7 minutes.

Transfer the grilled asparagus to a serving platter. Scatter the tarragon leaves across the top and serve warm or at room temperature with the aioli on the side.

SKILLET ASPARAGUS WITH SCALLIONS AND PONZU

Makes 2 to 3 servings

I learned this technique of skillet cooking from one of Edna Lewis's simplest recipes. She described how to cook whole scallions in a hot skillet with a little fat, some salt, and a lid, trapping the heat and letting the existing moisture in the vegetables steam them from the inside. It's important to shake the pan periodically, so that the pieces making contact with the hot surface do not scorch, like making popcorn on the stove.

1 pound of asparagus

6 green onions

2 tablespoons toasted sesame oil

½ teaspoon kosher salt

1 tablespoon toasted sesame seeds

1 recipe Ponzu (page 31), or store-bought is fine

Line up the asparagus spears on a cutting board, and trim off the bottom 2 inches, or wherever they begin to get tough and woody. (The bottoms can be reserved to make Asparagus Bottom Soup on page 129.) Wash them well and pat dry. Slice the spears into 2-inch pieces on a bias.

If the outer layers of the green onions are weathered, remove them first, then trim the root ends and any wilted tops. Slice the green onions like the asparagus, into 2-inch pieces on a bias.

Place a 10-inch skillet over medium-high heat. Once hot, add the sesame oil and swirl to coat the bottom of the skillet. Add the asparagus and green onions to the pan, season with salt, and stir well to combine. Cover and cook for 1 minute, then shake the pan while holding the lid on and cook 1 minute more. Lift the lid and check for doneness. Continue cooking, uncovered, until the asparagus is tender but still crisp, up to 5 minutes more depending on the thickness of the stalks. Remove the pan from the heat and sprinkle the sesame seeds on top.

Serve warm from the skillet or transfer the mixture to a serving platter, with the ponzu on the side.

SAUTÉED SCALLOPS AND SWEET CORN WITH SAUCE VIERGE

Makes 4 servings

Here's a celebration of in-season ingredients with little manipulation. A luxurious one-skillet meal of juicy seared scallops and sweet summer corn is topped with what will soon be your new favorite fresh tomato sauce. Set yourself up for success by making the sauce vierge first, chopping the tomatoes and letting them mingle with herbs and olive oil while you sauté.

3 ears sweet corn

12 sea scallops

2 teaspoons kosher salt

1/4 teaspoon freshly ground white pepper

2 tablespoons extra virgin olive oil

1 tablespoon unsalted butter

1/4 cup chopped shallots

1/4 cup thinly sliced green onions

1/4 cup dry white wine

1 recipe Sauce Vierge (page 43)

Shuck the corn and discard the husks in the compost bin. Take a clean, dry towel and rub away any corn silk clinging to the surface and between the kernels. To remove the kernels from the cob, take a casserole dish or wide, shallow bowl and set a smaller bowl or large ramekin upside down in the center of the larger dish. Fold up a kitchen towel and place it on top of the upside down bowl. Rest a shucked corncob vertically on top of the towel. Slice the corn kernels off the cob with a chef's knife, letting them fall into the reservoir you created. Repeat with the remaining ears of corn.

Pat the scallops dry with paper towels and season them on both sides with 1 teaspoon of the salt and the white pepper.

Place a wide skillet over high heat. Add the oil and heat until it shimmers. Gently place the scallops in the hot pan and briefly shake the pan to prevent them from sticking on contact. Add the butter and cook until the scallops are nicely browned on the bottoms, 3 to 4 minutes. Flip the scallops and turn the heat off, but leave them in the pan to finish cooking, about 1 minute. When they are done, they will feel springy to the touch rather than firm. Transfer the scallops to a plate and set aside.

If there are any burnt or black bits in the pan, remove them with a slotted spoon, but leave the fat and juices from cooking the scallops in the pan. Return the heat to medium and add the shallots, green onions, and remaining 1 teaspoon salt. Cook, stirring often, until they begin to soften, about 1 minute. Stir in the corn and cook for 1 minute more, then add the white wine and scrape up any bits from the bottom of the pan using a wooden spoon. Cook until the wine has mostly evaporated, 3 to 4 minutes. Add the scallops, seared side up, and any juices that may have collected on the plate back to the pan to rewarm for about 1 minute. Transfer the corn and scallops to a serving platter or individual plates and top with a generous amount of the sauce vierge.

SPICE-RUBBED GRILLED CORN ON THE COB

Makes 4 servings

The popular grilled Mexican street corn elote may be more well known in the States, but there is a similar snack in India that is equally delicious. For this Indian-inspired version, grilled corn on the cob is slathered in butter and fragrant spices instead of mayonnaise and cheese. I love the textural contrast of the mustard seeds with the grilled corn, and the chile and ginger give it a nice hot kick.

4 ears sweet corn

1/2 cup ghee or unsalted butter

1 tablespoon ground cumin

1 teaspoon mustard seeds

1 jalapeño, minced

2 teaspoons minced fresh ginger

2 teaspoons freshly ground black pepper

1 teaspoon turmeric powder

1 teaspoon sweet paprika

Zest and juice of 1 lime

Flaky sea salt

Handful fresh cilantro leaves and thin stems, coarsely chopped

Heat the grill. If using gas, set to medium-high. If cooking over wood or charcoal, allow the flames to die down until the embers are glowing. If using a grill pan, place it over medium-high heat just before cooking.

Shuck the corn and discard the husks in the compost bin. Take a clean, dry towel and rub away any corn silk clinging to the surface and between the kernels.

Melt the ghee in a small skillet over medium heat. Add the cumin and mustard seeds and cook, swirling the pan, until they begin to sizzle, about 30 seconds. Decrease the heat to low and add the jalapeño, ginger, pepper, turmeric, and paprika. Cook while stirring constantly until aromatic and sizzling, about 1 minute. Remove the skillet from the heat and add the lime zest and juice. Set aside while you grill the corn.

Grill the corn until nicely charred on all sides, turning occasionally, about 10 minutes. (If you're using a grill pan, cook in batches and place a heavy skillet on top of the corn to weigh it down while cooking.) Transfer the grilled corn to a serving dish and spoon some of the spiced ghee over each ear, turning to coat evenly. Place the corn back on the grill and cook briefly on all sides until it sizzles and smells amazing, 2 to 3 minutes.

Return the corn to the serving dish and sprinkle generously with flaky sea salt and cilantro.

REALLY HERBACEOUS CREAMED CORN

Makes 4 to 6 servings

I am crazy about creamed corn but wanted to make a more vibrant version with lots of sweet, tender herbs and a touch of lemon to give it a lighter feel. Pureeing half of the corn in a food processor allows the volume of dairy to stay low, while still achieving that comforting creamy result.

4 ears sweet corn

3 tablespoons unsalted butter

1 sweet yellow onion, diced

2 teaspoons kosher salt

1/2 cup heavy cream

1/3 cup mixed fresh tender herbs, such as parsley, tarragon, fennel fronds, dill, basil, and chives

2 teaspoons fresh lemon juice

1/2 teaspoon freshly ground black pepper

Shuck the corn and remove the kernels from each cob following the instructions on page 133, reserving the cobs.

Place the corncobs in a medium pot and cover them with about 1 quart of water, or just enough to cover them. Bring to a boil over high heat. Decrease the heat to maintain a steady simmer and cook until the liquid takes on the flavor of the corn, about 40 minutes. Remove the cobs from the liquid and discard. Increase the heat to high and boil until the liquid is reduced to 1 cup.

Melt the butter in a 10-inch skillet over medium heat. Add the onions and season with 1 teaspoon of the salt. Cook, stirring occasionally, until the onions are translucent, 4 to 5 minutes. Add the corn kernels and the remaining 1 teaspoon salt and cook for another 4 to 5 minutes. Add the cream and corncob reduction and simmer until thickened, 10 to 12 minutes.

Remove the pan from the heat and transfer half of the cooked corn mixture to the bowl of a food processor. Blitz until a thick chunky paste forms, about 1 minute. Mix this back into the pan with the whole kernels and add the herbs, lemon juice, and pepper. Taste for seasoning and adjust as needed.

GRILLED OKRA "RIBS" WITH CHIPOTLE MAYO

Makes 4 to 6 servings

It can be challenging to grill smaller vegetables that risk falling through the grill grates. Yes, you can get a vegetable screen for grilling petite produce, but you don't get the direct contact with the hot grates or the flavor that comes with it. Plus, it's just one more thing to clean. By double skewering okra into "ribs," you'll have much more control when turning them over the coals, and if you like, you can serve them this way for a fun new presentation.

About 6 wooden skewers, soaked in water for 1 hour

1 pound fresh okra pods

2 tablespoons peanut oil

1½ teaspoons kosher salt

1 teaspoon ground cumin

½ teaspoon crushed red pepper

1 recipe Chipotle Mayo (page 14)

Heat the grill. If using gas, set to high. If cooking over wood or charcoal, allow the flames to die down until the embers are glowing. If using a grill pan, place it over medium-high heat just before cooking.

Arrange 6 of the okra pods side by side on your work surface with all tips facing the same direction. Holding the pods in place with one hand, thread a skewer about ½ inch from the top of each, leaving at least 1 inch free on either end of the skewer. Thread a second skewer about ½ inch from the tip of each pod. Repeat to thread all the okra onto the skewers in the same manner and place them all on a tray to take to the grill. Brush the okra with oil and sprinkle with the salt, cumin, and crushed red pepper.

Grill the okra, turning once, until lightly charred and tender but not mushy, 3 to 5 minutes per side. (If you're using a grill pan, cook in batches and place a heavy skillet on top of the okra skewers to weigh them down while cooking.) Transfer the grilled okra back to the tray and slip the pods off the skewers. Pile them on a platter and serve hot with the chipotle mayonnaise on the side for dipping.

SAVANNAH RED RICE

Makes 4 to 6 servings

Growing up in Savannah, red rice was a mainstay side dish at seafood shacks, Sunday suppers, and even the school cafeteria. A tomato-based broth is the foundation that brings varying levels of heat and it almost always has some smoked pork involved. It can be served plain, embellished with shrimp or crabmeat, or studded with sliced summer okra. Thinly sliced okra cooks quickly and still holds some of its crunch. It's tempting to peek on the rice once it's off the heat, but it is important to leave the lid on while it rests— this ensures that the heat and steam are trapped in to cook the grains evenly across the top.

4 tablespoons bacon fat, unsalted butter, or a combination of both

8 ounces smoked sausage, sliced on a bias into 1/2-inch-thick pieces

1 small yellow onion, diced

1 cup diced celery, including leaves

2 cloves garlic, minced

1 tablespoon plus 1 teaspoon kosher salt, plus more to taste

3 cups Seasonal Vegetable Stock or Roasted Chicken Stock (page 11), or store-bought is fine

One 14-ounce can crushed tomatoes, or 2 cups chopped fresh tomatoes

2 tablespoons apple cider vinegar

3 bay leaves

1 teaspoon dried thyme

1/2 teaspoon freshly ground black pepper

1/4 teaspoon cayenne pepper

2 cups Carolina gold rice or other medium-grain gold or white rice

8 ounces thinly sliced okra (about 2 cups)

In a medium saucepan, melt 2 tablespoons of the bacon fat or butter over medium heat. Add the sausage and cook until browned on all sides, 4 to 5 minutes. Using a slotted spoon, transfer the sausage to a plate and set aside, leaving the fat in the pan. To the pan, add the onions, celery, and garlic and season with 1 tablespoon of the salt. Cook until the vegetables are tender, stirring often, about 5 minutes. Add the stock, tomatoes, vinegar, bay leaves, thyme, black pepper, and cayenne and stir well to combine. Increase the heat to high and bring to a lively simmer. Decrease the heat to maintain a gentle simmer, partially cover, and cook for 15 to 20 minutes, stirring occasionally.

In a 10-inch cast-iron skillet, melt the remaining 2 tablespoons of bacon fat or butter over medium heat. Add the rice and cook in the hot fat, stirring constantly, until the rice turns opaque, 2 to 4 minutes. Carefully stir in 4 1/2 cups of the hot tomato mixture and 1/4 cup water and bring to a simmer. Decrease the heat to low, cover, and cook until the liquid is absorbed and the rice is almost tender, 20 to 25 minutes. Remove the skillet from the heat and set aside, covered, for 10 minutes to let the top of the rice finish steaming.

Add the okra and the remaining 1 teaspoon of salt to the saucepan with the remaining tomato sauce. Cook over medium-low heat until the okra is crisp-tender, about 5 minutes. Stir in the sausage and remove the pan from the heat. Lift the lid from the skillet of rice and add the okra-and-sausage mixture. Fluff it with a fork, tossing it all together. Taste for seasoning and adjust to your liking. (If some of the rice remains undercooked, place the skillet in a low oven, covered, for 10 to 15 minutes before serving.)

MARINATED ARTICHOKE HEARTS

Makes 1 quart

Preparing artichokes can feel like a big task for a small reward, but if you're doing several at a time you get your rhythm down and suddenly take joy in exposing the treasure inside. I like to marinate mature globe artichokes because they have larger, meaty hearts. These are great on a charcuterie board, awesome in salads, or could be the star of your next simple pasta dish. They store very well in the fridge for a long time, so you can enjoy them again and again.

3 lemons, halved

6 globe artichokes

1 tablespoon extra virgin olive oil

1 tablespoon fine sea salt

1 cup Garlic Oil (page 30)

²/₃ cup Champagne vinegar

1 teaspoon whole-grain mustard

1 teaspoon dried oregano

½ teaspoon crushed red pepper

2 bay leaves, preferably fresh ones

Heat the oven to 350°F.

Fill a large bowl with water and squeeze in the lemon juice. Hold on to the spent lemon rinds. For each artichoke, first snap off the leaves starting at the base. Cut off the top third of the tip and the weathered end of the stem. Switch to a paring knife to peel the outer layer of the base and stem to expose the more tender center. Cut the artichokes in half if small, or quarters if larger, and rub the entire exterior with the spent lemon halves. Dig out and discard the fuzzy choke with a spoon or paring knife and rub the interior with the lemons as well. Place each prepared artichoke heart in the bowl of lemon water as you go.

Drain the artichoke hearts from the lemon water. On a large rimmed baking sheet, toss them in the oil and ½ teaspoon of the salt and spread them out. Bake until they are tender when pierced with a paring knife, 25 to 30 minutes. Set aside to cool completely.

Meanwhile, in a small bowl, whisk ²/₃ cup water with the garlic oil, vinegar, mustard, oregano, crushed red pepper, bay leaves, and remaining 2½ teaspoons salt. Layer the artichokes in a quart jar and pour the marinade over them. Chill overnight before serving. They will keep in the refrigerator for up to 1 month, as long as they stay completely submerged with a layer of oil on top.

ARTICHOKES WITH CURRIED YOGURT

Makes 4 to 6 servings

A simple homemade curried yogurt sauce makes a delicious dip for steamed artichokes, and it's a fun and interactive dish to greet friends and family. If you can get your hands on some baby artichokes, use them for steaming in this method. They haven't yet developed the fuzzy thistle, so can be eaten whole for easy prep and snacking. Larger globe artichokes work as well, but require a little more prep before the party.

2 pounds baby artichokes or
6 globe artichokes

3 bay leaves

1 teaspoon A Simple Curry Powder
(page 4), or store-bought is fine

Flaky sea salt

Extra virgin olive oil

1 recipe Curried Yogurt (page 15)

Follow the instructions for prepping artichokes on page 145. If you're working with baby artichokes, there is likely no need to peel the base or stem, and a fuzzy choke may not be present.

Fill a large pot with 1 to 2 inches of water and add the bay leaves. Insert a steamer basket in the bottom and place the pot over high heat. Once the water reaches a boil, add the artichokes to the steamer basket and adjust the heat to maintain a gentle simmer. Cover the pot with a lid and steam until the base of each artichoke is tender when pierced with a paring knife. This will take 10 to 12 minutes for baby artichokes and 15 to 20 minutes for globe artichokes.

Remove the artichokes from the steamer basket and arrange them on a serving platter. Season them with the curry powder, some flaky sea salt, and a drizzle of olive oil. Serve the yogurt on the side for dipping.

BRASSICAS

It wasn't that long ago that cauliflower and Brussels sprouts were passed by, and now they are on everyone's shopping list. Brassicas are having a moment. It is one of the largest and most diverse botanical families, but in this section, I've included only those that form an edible head. Other brassicas come in the form of roots and leaves, so they've been highlighted in the corresponding chapters based on how they are used in the kitchen.

Broccoli, cauliflower, and romanesco all have fully formed heads that resemble little bonsai trees. The florets can be eaten raw, either shaved into a salad or grated into a couscous-like texture. I like to gently blanch them, which softens their edges while preserving their color. When high heat is applied, they become wonderfully charred and have a unique nutty flavor, with the complexity of both sweetness and bitterness. And don't forget the stalks: though they have a tough exterior, you can peel and prepare them however you would florets.

That distinct brassica flavor is perhaps most exemplified in the taste of Brussels sprouts and cabbage. Whether they are broiled in the oven or stir-fried in a wok, their pleasant funk still shines through. Take cabbage beyond the obvious slaw—wedges can be grilled like steaks, or the individual leaves can be softened to a pliable wrap for a savory filling.

Raab are the flowering buds of many brassica plants, and they make a special spring treat. Broccoli raab is most commonly found, but look for any raab from the brassica family at the farmers' market. They are wonderful roasted or grilled. I've also highlighted a unique way to cook bok choy that involves griddling to get caramelization while still maintaining the delicate integrity of its tender leaves and crisp, juicy core.

One of the most interesting plants in this family is kohlrabi. Hailing from Eastern Europe, this brassica is becoming a more popular find in the United States. It has a solid round head that grows just above the ground, with leafy offshoots that sprout from the sides. As with other brassicas, both parts are edible, and can be eaten raw or cooked.

BROILED BROCCOLI WITH HALLOUMI AND ZA'ATAR

Makes 6 servings

When cutting up a head of broccoli, compare it to the structure of a tree. If you were taking a tree down, you'd start at the trunk and then begin removing the branches. Cutting broccoli from the stem and then separating the florets leaves nice organic shapes that have surface texture, perfect for trapping a flurry of za'atar or a drizzle of good olive oil. When broiled along with the broccoli, salty halloumi brings that satisfying chewy texture and umami that rocks this dish to the next level.

1½ pounds broccoli

One 7- to 8-ounce block halloumi, cut into ¾-inch cubes

3 tablespoons extra virgin olive oil, plus more for drizzling

1 clove garlic, grated or pressed

½ teaspoon kosher salt

½ teaspoon crushed red pepper

Zest and juice of ½ lemon

1 tablespoon Za'atar (page 7), or store-bought is fine

Peel the fibrous outer layer from the broccoli stalks using a peeler or paring knife. Using a chef's knife, cut the crowns off of each stalk. Cut the crowns into florets where they naturally divide. If the florets are larger, cut them lengthwise into bite-size pieces and break them apart into natural shapes. Slice the thicker peeled stalks into bite-size pieces.

Heat the broiler to high with a rack positioned 6 to 8 inches below.

In a large bowl, toss the broccoli, halloumi, oil, garlic, salt, and crushed red pepper. Tip the mixture out onto a large rimmed baking sheet and spread it in a single layer. Broil until the halloumi is browned and melty, and the broccoli is crisp-tender and the edges are crispy or even lightly charred, 8 to 12 minutes.

Remove the pan from the oven and squeeze the lemon juice over everything. Sprinkle with the lemon zest and za'atar and drizzle with more olive oil, if desired. Serve warm or at room temperature.

BROCCOLI AND STEAK SALAD

Makes 4 to 6 servings

The flavors of Sicily inspired this entree salad, with green olives, fennel, citrus, and, of course, good olive oil. Thinly sliced raw broccoli has texture and crunch, and gets better as it sits, while the beef plays more of a supporting role. Pull this one together on a beautiful day that beckons for a spontaneous picnic, and pack the cooler with a chilled dark rosé or a light, fruity red.

One 12- to 14-ounce flank steak

1 tablespoon kosher salt, divided

1/2 teaspoon freshly ground black pepper

12 ounces broccoli or romanesco

1 medium fennel bulb, including stalks

1/2 cup pitted green olives, sliced

5 cloves Garlic Confit, thinly sliced, plus 6 tablespoons Garlic Oil (page 30)

2 tablespoons fresh lemon juice, plus 2 teaspoons finely grated lemon zest

2 teaspoons canola or grapeseed oil

1/2 teaspoon crushed red pepper

1/2 teaspoon ground fennel seed

Flaky sea salt for finishing

Good extra virgin olive oil for finishing

Season the steak evenly on both sides with 1½ teaspoons of the kosher salt and the black pepper. Set aside to come to room temperature while you prep the vegetables.

Remove the fibrous outer layer from the broccoli stalks using a peeler or paring knife. Cut each head into quarters through the stem. Shave each quarter on a mandoline or a sharp knife and place them in a large bowl. Throw in any tiny florets or pieces that broke off.

Trim the stalks from the fennel bulb and thinly slice them crosswise. Slice the bulb as you did the broccoli. Add the fennel, olives, and garlic confit to the broccoli. Toss with the garlic oil, lemon juice and zest, and remaining 1½ teaspoons of kosher salt and set aside while you sear the steak.

Place a cast-iron skillet over medium-high heat. Turn on the hood vent or open a window. Once the pan is hot, add the canola or grapeseed oil and carefully place the steak in the skillet. Sear the meat until it is nicely charred, 3 to 4 minutes per side, lowering the heat as needed if the skillet starts to smoke. Transfer the steak to a plate to rest for 5 to 10 minutes.

Thinly slice the steak against the grain on a bias. Reserve any juices that are released from the steak and toss them into the salad.

Pile the salad onto a serving platter and shingle pieces of the sliced beef on top. Sprinkle everything with the crushed red pepper, ground fennel seed, and some flaky sea salt, and drizzle generously with extra virgin olive oil.

CAULIFLOWER CHAAT

4 to 6 servings

Chaat is a ubiquitous Indian street food that combines layers upon layers of contrasting flavors and textures. The components span savory and sweet, tangy and fatty, crunchy and creamy, creating a dynamic experience on the palate. This vegetable version celebrates cauliflower as a blank canvas for tart yogurt, sweet chutney, curry spice, fried shallots, pistachios, and pomegranate.

1 large or 2 small heads cauliflower (about 2 pounds)

1 tablespoon A Simple Curry Powder (page 4), or store-bought is fine

½ teaspoon freshly ground black pepper

2 tablespoons coconut oil, melted

1 tablespoon fresh lemon juice

2 teaspoons kosher salt

1 cup plain yogurt

½ cup Quick Coconut-Cilantro Chutney (page 31), or a store-bought Indian-style chutney like mango or tamarind

½ cup pomegranate seeds

½ cup roasted nuts, such as peanuts, cashews, or pistachios (see page 24), coarsely chopped

½ cup Crispy Fried Shallots (page 26)

½ cup coarsely chopped cilantro

Heat the broiler with a rack in the top position of the oven.

Quarter the head of the cauliflower through the core. Cut each quarter into florets or large bite-size pieces and place them on a rimmed baking sheet. Sprinkle the curry powder and black pepper over the cauliflower and add the coconut oil, lemon juice, and salt. Toss it all together to coat the cauliflower evenly.

Broil until the cauliflower is tender and nicely browned, 8 to 12 minutes, turning it over on the pan halfway through. Remove from the oven and let cool, then taste for seasoning.

Spread the yogurt in the center of individual serving plates or one large platter. Pile the roasted cauliflower over the yogurt and top with the chutney, pomegranate seeds, roasted nuts, fried shallots, and cilantro.

CAULIFLOWER SALAD WITH CELERY, DRIED APRICOTS, AND PISTACHIOS

Makes 4 to 6 servings

Riced cauliflower has had a moment, and although it's now easy to purchase in that form, it's just as easy and more economical to make it yourself. It takes just a moment to grate on a box grater or pulse in the food processor, and the resulting rice-like grains of raw cauliflower make the base for a texturally intriguing salad. I used to make this salad with cooked rice, but when I tried the cauliflower version, I liked it even more.

1 head cauliflower
(about 1½ pounds)

2 cups diced celery

1 cup dried apricots, chopped

½ cup chopped roasted pistachios
(see page 24)

1 recipe Sumac Vinaigrette
(page 19)

½ teaspoon kosher salt

Peel away and discard any green leaves attached to the base of the cauliflower. Cut the head in half through the core. Holding the stem end of one of the halves, grate the cauliflower on the large holes of a box grater. Repeat with the second half. Any pieces that fall off can be finely chopped and added to the pile.

In a large bowl, combine the grated cauliflower, celery, apricots, and pistachios. Add the vinaigrette and salt and toss together until well combined. Taste for seasoning and adjust to your liking.

ROMANESCO CAMPANELLE WITH WHITE BOLOGNESE

Makes 6 to 8 servings

This is one of those comforting dishes that is like a warm hug in a bowl. Red bolognese sauce goes all white using parsnips or turnips in place of the carrot, turkey or chicken in place of the beef, and a light herby cream sauce rather than tomato. Ruffled, cone-shaped campanelle pasta traps in all the tasty bits. Romanesco, that stunning fractal hybrid of broccoli and cauliflower, eats more like tender chunks of meat here. The result is an incredibly flavorful cold-weather pasta dish.

4 tablespoons unsalted butter

1 cup diced yellow onion

1 cup diced celery

1 1/2 cups diced parsnips, turnips, or (better yet) a combination

1/4 cup plus 2 teaspoons kosher salt

1 pound ground turkey or chicken

1 tablespoon chopped garlic

1 tablespoon chopped fresh rosemary

1 tablespoon chopped fresh sage

1 tablespoon chopped fresh oregano

1/2 teaspoon crushed red pepper

1/2 teaspoon freshly ground black pepper

2 cups Roasted Chicken Stock (page 11), or store-bought is fine

2 cups half-and-half, or 1 cup heavy cream plus 1 cup whole milk

1 large head romanesco or broccoli (about 1 1/2 pounds)

1 pound campanelle or similarly sized dried pasta

1 cup freshly grated Parmigiano-Reggiano cheese, plus more for finishing

In a Dutch oven, melt the butter over medium heat. Add the onions, celery, parsnips and/or turnips, and 1 teaspoon of the salt. Cook, stirring often, until the vegetables are softened, about 10 minutes. Transfer the vegetables to a bowl using a slotted spoon and set aside. Add the ground meat to the hot pan and use the back of a spoon to press it down in an even, flat layer. Season with 1 teaspoon of the salt, and let it cook undisturbed to brown on the bottom, 4 to 5 minutes. Break up the meat into small chunks and stir vigorously to evenly brown, 1 to 2 minutes. Add the vegetables back to the pan, along with the garlic, rosemary, sage, oregano, crushed red pepper, and black pepper. Cook, stirring often, until the mixture is aromatic and the garlic is lightly toasted, 2 to 3 minutes. Pour in the chicken stock and half-and-half and bring to a simmer. Adjust the heat to maintain a gentle simmer, stirring often, for 25 to 30 minutes.

Meanwhile, bring 4 quarts of water to a boil in a large pot over high heat and add the remaining 1/4 cup of salt.

Trim the base of the romanesco and remove any outer leaves. Cut the florets from the core. Dice the core and cut the florets into bite-size pieces. When the water comes to a boil, add the romanesco and cook until crisp-tender, about 3 minutes. Using a slotted spoon, transfer the blanched romanesco to a baking sheet and set aside.

Let the water return to a boil. Add the pasta, stir well, and cook until al dente according to the package directions. Reserve about 1 cup of the cooking water and drain the pasta in a colander.

Add the pasta and romanesco to the hot bolognese sauce and toss to coat well. Add the cheese and just enough of the reserved cooking water to create a velvety sauce. Spoon the pasta into warm bowls and sprinkle with more freshly grated cheese.

ROASTED BRUSSELS SPROUTS WITH BEURRE ROUGE AND ALMONDS

Makes 4 servings

My favorite way to cook Brussels sprouts is very quickly with high heat, caramelizing the exterior to bring out sweetness while leaving the interior tender but still with a little bite. Beurre rouge sauce is super old-school French cookery at its best and worth revisiting. It adds a welcome drizzle of fat and acid to the sweet sprouts. Toasted almonds add a nutty crunch that ties it all together.

1 pound Brussels sprouts

3 shallots, halved and thinly sliced lengthwise

3 cloves garlic, thinly sliced

3 tablespoons extra virgin olive oil

2 teaspoons kosher salt

1/2 teaspoon freshly ground black pepper

1/2 cup roasted slivered almonds (see page 24)

1 recipe Beurre Rouge (page 38)

Heat the oven to 450°F.

Trim the base of each Brussels sprout and cut them in half lengthwise if small or into quarters if they are larger. Place the Brussels sprouts, and any loose leaves left on the cutting board, into a bowl and add the shallots and garlic. Add the oil, salt, and pepper and toss well to combine.

Turn the mixture out onto a large rimmed baking sheet and roast until just tender and some of the leaves begin to brown, 8 to 10 minutes. If you'd like more caramelization, switch the oven to broil on high and cook for 2 to 4 minutes until the desired color is achieved.

Pile the Brussels sprouts and all the bits from the bottom of the baking sheet onto a serving platter and sprinkle with the almonds. Drizzle the beurre rouge over it all and serve warm.

STIR-FRIED BRUSSELS SPROUTS WITH FISH SAUCE AND LIME

Makes 4 servings

Finely chopped Brussels sprouts might take a little time on the cutting board, but the stir-frying part moves quickly. The smell of the hot, sizzling sprouts cooking in the blistering wok, with fish sauce, ginger, and lime, is intoxicating. This dish will bring a nice punch of flavor alongside simply cooked chicken and steamed rice.

1 pound Brussels sprouts

Juice of 1 lime, plus more to taste

1 tablespoon fish sauce, plus more to taste

1 tablespoon dark brown sugar

2 tablespoons vegetable oil

2 shallots, halved and thinly sliced

4 green onions, white and green parts thinly sliced

One 1-inch piece ginger, peeled and cut into matchsticks

1 Thai chile, thinly sliced

1 teaspoon kosher salt

Trim the base of each Brussels sprout, and cut them in half lengthwise, keeping any loose leaves that fall onto the cutting board as you go. Place the halves cut side down and thinly slice them lengthwise. If a piece becomes too small to safely continue slicing, try flipping it over to the other cut side for more leverage, and just get it as thin as you can into even shavings. (Accuracy doesn't count here; texture does.)

In a small bowl, mix the lime juice, fish sauce, and sugar until dissolved and set the sauce near the stove.

Now be prepared to work quickly, as this recipe moves fast. Place a wok or a well-seasoned cast-iron skillet over medium-high heat and add the vegetable oil. When the oil begins to shimmer, add the shallots, green onions, ginger, chile, and salt and cook, stirring constantly with a wok spatula or wooden spoon, until they begin to brown, 1 to 2 minutes. Add the Brussels sprouts and continue to toss the ingredients up from the bottom of the pan to keep it all moving. Cook, tossing often, until the Brussels sprouts are a little wilted but still crisp-tender, 3 to 4 minutes. Add the sauce and stir to combine. Cook for about 1 minute, then remove the pan from the heat. Taste for seasoning and adjust with more lime juice or fish sauce, as you'd like.

SAVOY CABBAGE ROLLS WITH MUSHROOMS AND FARRO

Makes 4 to 6 servings

This is my vegetarian take on Eastern European stuffed cabbage. Mushrooms bring meatiness, so you don't miss the ground pork or beef, and farro adds nuttiness and texture beyond the usual white rice. I suggest a head of savoy cabbage, with more pliable leaves for rolling, but because they are ruffled and ruched they kind of interlock with one another. Take care in pulling them apart to fill.

2/3 cup farro

1/4 cup plus 4 teaspoons kosher salt

1 head Savoy cabbage

1/4 cup extra virgin olive oil

8 ounces mushrooms, such as oyster, cremini, or chanterelle, finely chopped

2 medium carrots, cut into 1/4-inch cubes

2 stalks celery, cut into 1/4-inch cubes

1 yellow onion, cut into 1/4-inch dice

1 tablespoon chopped fresh rosemary

One 28-ounce can crushed tomatoes

1/2 cup dry red wine

Thinly sliced chives for garnish

In a medium saucepan, combine 3 cups of water, the farro, and 1 teaspoon of the salt. Place it over high heat and bring to a boil. Decrease the heat to maintain a simmer and cook until the farro is tender and pleasantly chewy, 25 to 30 minutes. Check it often toward the end of the cooking time, and add a little more water if it becomes too dry. When done, drain the farro in a fine-mesh sieve and set aside.

Bring 4 quarts of water to a boil in a large pot over high heat and season with 1/4 cup of the salt. Line a large rimmed baking sheet with a clean kitchen towel and set it near the stove.

With the tip of a knife, cut around the core of the cabbage to free the outer leaves. Carefully pull apart the leaves, making sure to keep them whole. You should have 12 leaves that are large enough to fill. Reserve any extra leaves and the smaller, inner part of the head for another use. Working in batches if needed, blanch the cabbage leaves in the boiling water until they are pliable, 4 to 5 minutes. Carefully remove the leaves with tongs and spread them out on the prepared baking sheet to cool.

Heat the oven to 350°F. In a medium pot, heat 2 tablespoons of the oil over medium heat. Add the mushrooms and 1 teaspoon of the salt and cook, stirring often, until lightly browned, about 5 minutes. Transfer the mushrooms to a plate.

To the pot, add 1 tablespoon of the oil, the carrots, celery, onions, rosemary, and 1 teaspoon of the salt. Cook, stirring occasionally, until the vegetables begin to soften, 4 to 5 minutes. Add the crushed tomatoes, wine, and remaining 1 teaspoon of salt and bring to a simmer. Cook until the vegetables are tender, about 15 minutes. Remove the sauce from the heat and set aside.

In a large bowl, mix the cooked mushrooms, farro, and 1 cup of the tomato sauce to make the stuffing. Spread 1 cup of the remaining tomato sauce in a large shallow baking dish to coat the bottom. Fill each cabbage leaf with 1/3 to 1/2 cup of the stuffing. Wrap the leaf around the filling and roll it up like a burrito, tucking the edges in as you go. Place each stuffed cabbage leaf in the baking dish seam side down. Once all the leaves are stuffed, cover them with the remaining sauce.

Place the baking dish on the middle rack of the oven and bake until hot, about 30 minutes. Sprinkle the cabbage rolls with chives before serving.

GRILLED RED CABBAGE SALAD

Makes 6 to 8 servings

Grilling cabbage takes this sturdy brassica into new territory. Because the leaves are so tightly crammed together on the head, you get two different textures, which is what I like most about this method: the outer leaves become charred and wilted, while the inner ones get steamed from their own moisture but retain some crunch. You can play around with how long to char the cabbage for a deeper or lighter flavor, and a more tender versus firm texture within. The crisp apples and hazelnuts in this dish build upon these flavors and textures and play nicely with the warm mustard seed vinaigrette.

1 small red cabbage (about 1½ pounds)

1 bunch green onions, root ends trimmed

¼ cup plus 1 tablespoon canola or vegetable oil

4 teaspoons kosher salt

¼ cup apple cider vinegar

2 teaspoons yellow mustard seeds

2 teaspoons brown mustard seeds (or substitute with more yellow mustard seeds)

2 tart-sweet apples, such as honeycrisp, pink lady, or Fuji, chopped

½ cup roasted hazelnuts (see page 24), coarsely chopped

1 tablespoon honey

1 tablespoon Dijon mustard

Heat the grill. If using gas, set to medium. If cooking over wood or charcoal, allow the flames to die down until the embers are glowing. If using a grill pan, place it over medium heat just before cooking.

Trim the exposed end of the cabbage core and quarter the head lengthwise through the core into wedges, leaving the interior core intact to hold the wedges together. Place the wedges on a large rimmed baking sheet along with the green onions. Rub all sides of the cabbage and the onions with 1 tablespoon of the oil. Sprinkle them with 2 teaspoons of the salt.

Place the cabbage wedges on the grill and cook on all sides (the two cut sides and the rounded outer side) until nicely charred, 8 to 10 minutes per side. The interior leaves will still be firm but warm. Transfer the grilled cabbage wedges back to the rimmed baking sheet.

Next grill the green onions, turning occasionally, until wilted and lightly charred, 2 to 4 minutes. Transfer the green onions to the baking sheet with the grilled cabbage and set aside until both are cool enough to handle.

Meanwhile, in a small saucepan, combine the vinegar, yellow and brown mustard seeds, and remaining 2 teaspoons of salt. Slowly bring to a lively simmer over medium-low heat, then immediately remove the pan from the heat. Cover and set aside for 15 minutes to bloom the mustard seeds while you prepare the salad.

When the cabbage and green onions are slightly cooled, cut away and discard the core from each cabbage wedge and coarsely tear or chop the leaves. Pile the leaves on a serving platter. Cut the green onions into 1-inch pieces and scatter them over the cabbage. Scatter the apples and hazelnuts over the top.

Uncover the vinegar mixture and whisk in the remaining oil, honey, and mustard. Return the pan to medium-high heat and bring the mixture to a boil. Immediately remove the pan from the heat and spoon the hot dressing over the salad. Serve warm or at room temperature.

CRUNCHY KOHLRABI SALAD WITH ROASTED ALMONDS

Makes 4 servings

If you have never eaten raw kohlrabi, it kind of reminds me of the structure of jicama with the flavor of broccoli. One of the things I think about most when cooking is texture, and this is a simple recipe all about that crunch. Kohlrabi are sometimes available with tops, and you should totally incorporate them into this salad if they are still attached. If they've been lopped off, oh well. Use skin-on almonds for this recipe to give it even more character.

1½ pounds kohlrabi, preferably with tops attached

½ cup roasted skin-on almonds (see page 24), coarsely chopped

2 teaspoons fresh lemon juice, plus more to taste

3 tablespoons extra virgin olive oil

1 teaspoon flaky sea salt, plus more to taste

If the kohlrabi tops are present, trim them at the base of each stem where they attach to the bulb and set aside. Peel each kohlrabi bulb, being sure to remove enough of the outer layer to reach the white, less-fibrous center, and cut or peel away any areas that feel tough or woody. Cut the peeled bulbs into ⅓-inch-thick planks, then lay the planks flat and cut them into batons. Cut the longer pieces in half on the bias, so they are all about the same length, and place the pieces in a medium bowl.

If using the tops, stack them on the cutting board, lining up the leaves and stems. Beginning at the ends of the stems, thinly slice them crosswise, working up to the leaves. Continue slicing the leaves crosswise into ⅓-inch-thick ribbons. Add tops and stems to the bowl with the batons.

Add the almonds, lemon juice, oil, and salt to the bowl and toss it all together. Taste for seasoning and adjust to your liking, adding more lemon juice or salt as you like.

RAAB AND WHITE BEANS ON TOAST

Makes 2 to 4 servings

In the springtime, many brassicas grow shoots that have flower buds at the end, which are wonderfully tender and tasty. I like to make them a little spicy with crushed red pepper and serve them over white beans spread on a crusty baguette. Most commonly you'll see broccoli raab at the farmers' market, but look out for the shoots from collards and kale too. Broccolini from the grocery store will work well here too. Make this for a quick lunch, a snack before dinner, or as an accompaniment to a soup supper.

4 tablespoons extra virgin olive oil, plus more for drizzling

1 cup diced yellow onion

1 tablespoon minced garlic

½ teaspoon crushed red pepper

2 teaspoons kosher salt

1¾ cups cooked cannellini beans (canned or home-cooked), cooking liquid reserved

1 bunch raab

½ baguette

1 lemon, quartered and seeds removed

Shaved Parmigiano-Reggiano or Pecorino Romano cheese for finishing

In a medium skillet, heat 2 tablespoons of the oil over medium heat. Add half of the onions, half of the garlic, half of the crushed red pepper, and half of the salt. Cook, stirring frequently, until the onions are translucent and the ingredients are beginning to brown, about 5 minutes. Add the cooked beans and ½ cup of the cooking liquid and bring to a simmer. Cook at a gentle simmer, adjusting the heat as needed, until the beans are heated through and the liquid thickens, about 5 minutes. Splash in more of the liquid or water if the mixture becomes too dry. Using a potato masher, crush the beans to create a chunky spread. Remove the pan from heat and taste for seasoning. Adjust to your liking and set aside.

Heat the broiler to high with a rack positioned 6 to 8 inches below.

Trim away the tough ends from the raab stems and pile the raab on a large rimmed baking sheet. Toss with 1 tablespoon of the oil and the remaining half of the onions, garlic, crushed red pepper, and salt. Spread it out in an even layer to the edges of the baking sheet. Broil until there is some slight browning on the greens and the ingredients on the bottom of the pan are sizzling, 6 to 10 minutes, stirring once halfway through. Remove the pan from the oven, leaving the broiler on, and set aside.

Cut the baguette half in half lengthwise so you have two long pieces of bread. Brush the cut sides with the remaining 1 tablespoon of oil and place under the broiler until lightly browned, hot, and crusty, 2 to 3 minutes.

Spread the beans over each half of the baguette, dividing it evenly. Arrange the raab evenly and randomly across the top of the beans as well as any bits left on the pan. You can cut the toasts into smaller segments to share or leave them whole. Finish by squeezing some lemon juice over each toast and drizzling with a little more olive oil, then top with some shaved cheese.

GRIDDLED BABY BOK CHOY WITH ORANGE AND COCONUT

Makes 4 servings

Bok choy is so crisp when raw but has such a high water content that it quickly becomes wilted and bogged with traditional steaming and sautéing techniques. This method of caramelizing bok choy halves on a hot griddle builds unexpected depth and dimension. Let the bok choy do its thing on the hot surface, caramelizing to a deep brown, while you pull the sauce and toppings together. Served alongside steamed fish and rice, it shines.

1 pound baby bok choy
(about 4 to 5 heads)

¼ cup peanut oil

2 teaspoons kosher salt

2 oranges, such as blood oranges, cara cara, navel, or a mix

3 green onions, thinly sliced

2 tablespoons unseasoned rice vinegar

1 teaspoon grated ginger

¼ cup unsweetened toasted coconut flakes (see page 24)

Trim the base of each bok choy and cut them in half lengthwise. Rinse well under cold running water, then shake off any excess water and pat dry. Place the halved sections of bok choy cut side up, drizzle all with 1 tablespoon of the oil, and sprinkle with 1 teaspoon of the salt.

Place a 12-inch cast-iron or other heavy skillet over medium-low heat and let it preheat for a few minutes. Add 1 tablespoon of oil and swirl to coat the bottom of the pan. Place the bok choy cut sides down in the pan in a single layer, with the whiter, bulby bottoms touching the pan and the green tops draped over them or in between them wherever they fit. (If they don't all fit in the pan in a single layer, cook them in two batches.) Let the bok choy cook relatively slowly on the surface of the hot skillet, without turning, until the cut sides are evenly browned and the leaves have wilted, 12 to 15 minutes. If after 10 minutes they are not yet beginning to brown, increase the heat a little. You may also need to move them around in the pan for even cooking. Once the bok choy are nicely caramelized on the cut sides, remove the pan from the heat.

Meanwhile, supreme the oranges. To do so, slice off the top and bottom of each orange with a paring knife and place one cut side down on the cutting board. Using the tip of the knife, carve away the skin and pith until the flesh is exposed and no white pith remains. Working over a bowl, hold the fruit in the palm of your hand and cut out each orange segment between the membranes, letting the segments drop into the bowl. When finished, squeeze the membrane over the bowl to extract the remaining juices. Discard the skin, pith, and membrane and pick out any seeds in the orange segments. Repeat with the other orange, then strain the juice from the segments and reserve it in a separate bowl.

In a small bowl, combine 2 tablespoons of the fresh orange juice with the green onions, vinegar, ginger, and remaining 1 teaspoon of salt. Whisk in the remaining 2 tablespoons of peanut oil. Taste the dressing for seasoning and adjust as needed.

Arrange the warm bok choy cut sides up on a platter and drizzle with the dressing. Top with the orange segments and toasted coconut.

LEGUMES

Edible pods and pulses comprise the large legume family. I'm talking about beans and peas here, in all their forms. They can be young, green pods; freshly shelled tender morsels; dried until hard; or ground into flour for later use.

Spring green legumes—like English peas, favas, sugar snaps, and snow peas—are the first to emerge in the season and tend to have more sweet vegetal flavors. They are prized for their delicateness, and for that reason, I prefer them barely cooked or raw. Some ideal ways to serve these seasonal treasures are in a simple pasta dish, lightly dressed for a salad, or briefly stir-fried or sautéed.

String beans, wax beans, pole beans, bush beans, and snap beans—regardless of what these edible pods are called in the field, in the kitchen they can basically be treated the same way. The subtle differences lie in whether or not they have strings that need to be removed, and if they are slightly more tough or tender, which dictates how long to cook them.

To string a bean, snap off the tip and pull down toward the outer seam to reveal and remove the string. If no string is revealed, you're good to go. Bush bean varieties lean toward the smaller, tender side (think haricots verts) and are well-suited for eating raw, blanching, or sautéing. Pole beans, named so for the pole needed to prop up the wandering vines, tend to have a longer pod and sometimes a tougher texture, so they benefit from the higher heat of grilling and roasting with fantastic results.

Shelling peas or beans—like black-eyed peas, crowders, zippers, white acres, cranberry beans, and butter beans (aka baby limas)—can be found freshly shucked. Fresh ones are only available in the warmer months and take less time to simmer than their dried counterparts. Butter beans, for instance, can be pureed into a smooth green hummus, and black-eyed peas can be shallow-fried until crispy.

Some legumes such as lentils, chickpeas, black beans, pintos, and gigantes are most commonly found dried. Many benefit from a long soak prior to cooking, to rehydrate them gradually and maintain their textural integrity. They can then be slowly simmered on the stove or cooked quickly in a pressure cooker. These legumes can be enjoyed simply with their pot likker, added to a sumptuous winter stew, or dressed in a vinaigrette for a hearty summer salad.

PAN-FRIED FISH WITH MINTED PEAS AND MALT VINEGAR MAYO

Makes 4 servings

British pub fish and chips is often served with mushy peas, but at home, fried fish with this puree of English peas flavored with mint, sans fries, is more practical and flavorful. Herbs add a wonderful dimension to the rustic mash. Use whatever beer you have in the fridge to make the batter, which results in a light and airy crust that holds its crunch. Whip up the malt vinegar aioli to slather on the fish and be sure to mix a little into each bite of the peas too.

MINTED PEAS

1 pound shelled English peas (about 2½ pounds of peas in pods)

2 tablespoons unsalted butter

2 tablespoons extra virgin olive oil

1 cup sliced spring onions or green onions

2 teaspoon kosher salt, plus more as needed

¼ teaspoon freshly ground black pepper

¼ cup flat-leaf parsley leaves

½ cup mint leaves

PAN-FRIED FISH

6 cups canola or vegetable oil

1½ cups all-purpose flour

1 tablespoon kosher salt

¾ teaspoon freshly ground black pepper

½ teaspoon paprika

1 egg, beaten

1 cup cold beer (whatever kind you like to drink)

Four 5- to 6-ounce cod or haddock fish filets

1 recipe Malt Vinegar Mayo (page 14)

Lemon wedges for serving

Beer for serving

FOR THE PEAS: Taste the peas and if they are sweet when raw, you can skip to the next step. If they are starchy, blanch them in a pot of lightly salted water until just tender and sweet, about 2 minutes.

In a medium skillet, heat the butter and olive oil over medium heat. Add the spring onions and salt, and cook until they are tender and beginning to brown, about 5 minutes. Add the peas and pepper, decrease the heat to medium-low, and place a lid on the skillet. Cook, covered but stirring occasionally, until the peas are tender but not mushy and still bright green, 6 to 7 minutes. Transfer the pea mixture to a food processor and add the parsley, mint, and ¼ cup water. Process to a coarse puree, 1 to 2 minutes. If the mixture is too thick to move freely in the food processor, add just enough water to get it moving while the motor is running. Taste for seasoning and adjust as needed. Turn the pea mixture out into a bowl and set aside until you're ready to serve or cover and chill for up to 1 day.

FOR THE FISH: Heat the oil in a deep, 6-quart Dutch oven until it reaches 350ºF on a deep-frying thermometer, then adjust the heat as needed to maintain that temperature while frying. Line a baking tray with paper towels and place it near the stove.

Combine the flour, 1½ teaspoons of the salt, ½ teaspoon of the pepper, and the paprika in a medium bowl. Transfer about half of the flour mixture to a shallow dish for dredging and set aside. Add the egg and beer to the bowl with the other half of the flour mixture and briefly stir it together with a fork; it's best to leave the beer batter a little lumpy to avoid overmixing.

Season each piece of fish with the remaining 1½ teaspoons of salt and ¼ teaspoon of pepper. One at a time, dredge each filet in the flour mixture, coating it evenly, then dip them into the beer batter. Carefully lower the fish into the hot oil; depending on the width of your pot, you may need to fry the fish in two batches. Let the fish cook for 5 to 6 minutes then carefully turn them over using a fish spatula or slotted spoon and continue to cook on the other side for another 5 to 6 minutes. Monitor the temperature of the oil closely and adjust as needed to maintain 350ºF. The coating should be golden brown and crisp and the internal temperature of the fish should reach 145ºF when it is done. Transfer the fried fish filets to the prepared tray as they are done. Serve alongside the peas, with the mayo, lots of lemon wedges, and your favorite beer.

PEAS AND RAMPS WITH MUSHROOMS AND SEMOLINA GNOCCHI

Makes 4 to 6 servings

I've never been very good at making a pillowy potato-based gnocchi dough, so when I discovered gnocchi alla Romana made from semolina, I knew I'd found my foolproof style. The semolina is cooked in a pot like polenta, then cooled and simply cut into disks. Traditionally it is finished in the oven, perhaps with tomato sauce, and topped with grated cheese to serve as a side dish. Here, the semolina gnocchi is a vessel for a sauté of spring peas, ramps, and mushrooms and fit for the role of main dish. Be sure to first taste the fresh peas raw. If they are a little starchy, they should be blanched to turn that blandness sweet. If you cannot find ramps, a wild foraged allium, you can use green onions or leeks instead.

4 tablespoons butter, plus more for greasing

4 cups whole milk

1 cup semolina flour, plus more for dusting

1 tablespoon kosher salt

1½ cups freshly grated Parmigiano-Reggiano cheese

1 teaspoon freshly ground black pepper

1 egg yolk

2 tablespoons extra virgin olive oil

8 ounces oyster mushrooms, torn into large bite-size pieces

2½ cups shelled English peas

1 bunch ramps or green onions, sliced

Grease a 13-by-9-inch baking dish with butter and line the bottom with a sheet of parchment paper that hangs over each of the two longer sides of the dish like wings; set aside.

In a medium saucepan, warm the milk over medium heat. When the milk just begins to steam, whisk in the measured semolina, 2 teaspoons of the salt, and the butter until smooth. Cook, stirring almost constantly with a wooden spoon, until the mixture becomes very thick and begins to subtly pull away from the sides of the pan, about 10 minutes. Remove the pan from the heat and stir in 1 cup of the cheese and ½ teaspoon of the pepper. Continue stirring until the cheese is melted, then add the egg yolk and stir until it is fully incorporated. Tip the mixture into the prepared baking dish and spread it in an even layer, about ½ inch thick. Cover tightly with plastic film and refrigerate until set, about 2 hours. (The dough can be made up to 2 days ahead.)

Heat the oven to 375ºF with a rack in the top position. Lift the chilled gnocchi dough from the baking dish using the parchment wings and transfer it to a cutting board. Clean out the baking dish and grease it with more butter (no parchment this time).

Using a cookie or biscuit cutter, or the rim of a drinking glass, cut the dough into 2-inch disks, dusting the cutter in a little semolina flour between cuts to prevent the dough from sticking. Arrange the disks in the greased baking dish in an overlapping single layer, like fish scales. After cutting as many disks as you can, wet your hands and gather the dough scraps back together. Pat and press them into a smooth ½-inch layer to cut more disks. Continue to gather the scraps of dough and reshape them to cut as many disks as possible, arranging them in the baking dish as you go.

Bake on the top rack of the oven until the gnocchi are hot, about 20 minutes. Switch to broil and continue cooking until the tops of the gnocchi are nicely browned at the edges, 3 to 5 minutes. Remove the dish from the oven and immediately sprinkle with the remaining ½ cup cheese.

Continue to next page for the rest of the recipe

Meanwhile, heat the oil in a wide skillet over medium-high heat until it shimmers. Add the mushrooms and season them with ½ teaspoon each of the remaining salt and pepper. Cook without disturbing the mushrooms until they are lightly browned on the bottom, about 2 minutes, then turn them over with tongs and brown on the other side, 1 to 2 minutes more. Stir in the peas and ramps and season with the remaining ½ teaspoon of salt. Add a splash of water and scrape up the bits from the bottom of the pan. Decrease the heat to medium-low, cover, and cook for 1 to 2 minutes, shaking the pan while holding the lid from time to time, until the peas are warmed through and the ramps are wilted. Taste for seasoning and adjust to your liking. Spoon the peas and ramps over the baked gnocchi at the table.

GREEN BUTTER BEAN HUMMUS

Makes about 3 cups

There are many colloquial terms for different beans and peas, depending on the region where you live. In the South, a butter bean is synonymous with a fresh baby lima bean. They are small with a soft green color and a starchy texture, perfect for whipping up into jade-hued hummus flavored with fresh thyme. Serve the hummus drizzled with olive oil and alongside your crudités or warm pita.

¼ cup kosher salt, plus more to taste

1 pound shelled green butter beans

⅓ cup tahini

¼ cup extra virgin olive oil

2 tablespoons fresh lemon juice, plus more to taste

3 cloves garlic, chopped

1 teaspoon fresh thyme leaves

Bring 3 quarts of water to a boil in a medium pot over high heat and add the salt. Add the butter beans and simmer until tender, 20 to 25 minutes, skimming any foam that rises to the surface as they cook. Drain the beans in a colander, reserving ½ cup of the cooking liquid.

Transfer the warm beans to a food processor and add the tahini, oil, lemon juice, garlic, and thyme. Puree until smooth, adding as much of the reserved water as needed to make a smooth, creamy hummus-like paste. Taste and add more salt or lemon juice, if desired. The hummus will keep in an airtight container in the refrigerator for up to 3 days. Bring to room temperature before serving.

SUGAR SNAP PEA SALAD

Makes 4 servings

Sweet sugar snaps are best celebrated in a simple salad. Here the snappy peas are tossed in an herby mustard vinaigrette and accented with fresh orange. It's a perfect picnic salad and brings freshness and crunch when served over grilled fish or glazed tofu.

2 tablespoons white balsamic vinegar

1 teaspoon whole-grain mustard

1 teaspoon chopped fresh dill

1 teaspoon kosher salt

3 tablespoons extra virgin olive oil

1 large orange, such as cara cara or Valencia

8 ounces sugar snap peas

In a mixing bowl, whisk the vinegar, mustard, dill, and salt. Drizzle in the oil while whisking to emulsify the vinaigrette.

Supreme the orange. To do so, slice off the top and bottom of each orange with a paring knife and place one cut side down on the cutting board. Using the tip of the knife, carve away the skin and pith until the flesh is exposed and no white pith remains. Working over the bowl of dressing, hold the fruit in the palm of your hand and cut out each orange segment between the membranes, letting the segments drop into the bowl. When finished, squeeze the membrane over the bowl to extract the juices. Discard the skin, pith, and membrane and any seeds.

To string peas (or beans), hold them in your hand with the stem end facing up. Snap off the tip toward one of the seams on either side and pull down the length of the legume. If there are strings, this action should reveal them, and they usually release as you pull down. Turn the legume over and repeat, snapping the other end and pulling down the opposite seam in the same motion to check the other side. (Some varieties of peas and beans are very stringy, while others are not, so I always check them first before preparing.)

Cut each pea pod in half on a bias and add them to the bowl with the oranges and dressing. Toss it all together, then taste for seasoning and adjust to your liking.

SNOW PEAS WITH MANGO, CHILE, AND SESAME

Makes 4 servings

Get all of your prep organized and be ready to go before you start cooking, as this stir-fry requires you to stay near the stove and move fast. The lithe snow peas and diced mango cook up quickly. Because there's a good bit of sugar in mango, a well-seasoned wok or cast-iron skillet is a must to keep the caramelizing fruit from sticking.

2 tablespoons canola oil

1 shallot, finely diced

1 small fresno chile, minced

2 tablespoons minced ginger

3 cloves garlic, minced

1½ teaspoons kosher salt

1 firm-ripe mango, peeled and diced

1 pound snow peas, tipped and strings removed (see page 187)

1 tablespoon fresh lime juice, plus more to taste

1 tablespoon toasted sesame oil

2 tablespoons toasted sesame seeds

1 large handful torn mint, basil, or a combination

Place a wok or a well-seasoned cast-iron skillet over medium-high heat and add the canola oil. When the oil starts to shimmer, add the shallots, chile, ginger, garlic, and salt and cook, stirring constantly with a wok spatula or wooden spoon, until they begin to brown, 2 to 3 minutes. Decrease the heat just a bit and add the mango. Stir like crazy, scraping the bottom of the pan to keep the mango from sticking. Add the snow peas and toss the ingredients up from the bottom to keep it all moving. Cook, tossing almost constantly, until the snow peas become more vibrant green in color, 2 to 3 minutes. Stir in the lime juice and sesame oil and remove the pan from the heat. Taste for seasoning and adjust to your liking. Garnish with the toasted sesame seeds and fresh herbs.

GRILLED POLE BEANS WITH PISTACHIO ROMESCO

Makes 6 servings

The name "pole bean" refers to the necessary support that the tall plant needs to grow, such as a trellis, a rigid pole, or even a sturdy cornstalk. Pole beans grow into a long edible pod that is hardier than its sibling, the bush bean. For grilling, I prefer romano beans or other Italian varieties that have a flat, wide shape, which makes them less susceptible to falling through the grill grates and into the flames. Note the no-turn grilling method for the beans, which lets them rest longer on one side to develop a deep char, while the other side stays a bit firmer.

1½ pounds pole beans, such as romano beans, tipped and strings removed (see page 187)

1 tablespoon extra virgin olive oil

1 teaspoon kosher salt

1 recipe Pistachio Romesco (page 42)

1 tablespoon chopped flat-leaf parsley

Heat the grill. If using gas, set to medium-high. If cooking over wood or charcoal, allow the flames to die down until the embers are glowing. If using a grill pan, place it over medium-high heat just before cooking.

In a shallow dish, rub the beans with the oil and sprinkle with the salt. Place the beans on the grill, arranging them perpendicular to the grates so they don't fall through. (If you're using a grill pan, cook in batches and place a heavy skillet on top of the beans to weigh them down while grilling.) Cover and cook until nicely charred on the bottom, 4 to 5 minutes, then remove them from the grill. The goal is to cook the beans just until tender but to char them on one side only.

Spread some of the romesco sauce onto a serving platter and pile the grilled beans on top. Garnish with chopped parsley.

AJIKA GREEN BEANS

Makes 6 to 8 servings

Ajika is a condiment from the Republic of Georgia that differs throughout the region but is typically made with walnuts, tomatoes, fresh or dried chiles, and various spices. It's incredibly fragrant, with deep, earthy flavors and a little kick. Rather than making a separate ajika sauce, I add the spices, tomato, and vinegar to the fresh tender green beans in stages, building the sauce in the pan.

3 tablespoons extra virgin olive oil

2 pounds green beans, tipped and strings removed (see page 187)

2½ teaspoons kosher salt

1 cup chopped roasted walnuts (see page 24)

1 shallot, diced

2 cloves garlic, minced

2 tablespoons Ajika Seasoning Blend (page 6), or store-bought is fine

1 cup diced tomato

1 tablespoon sherry vinegar

Chopped cilantro for garnish

Heat the oil in a wide skillet over medium heat. When it begins to shimmer, add the green beans and 1 teaspoon salt and toss with tongs to coat the beans in the oil. Add 1 tablespoon of water, cover, and cook, shaking the skillet vigorously over the heat for 1 to 2 minutes while holding the lid on. Uncover and toss the beans so the top layer makes contact with the bottom of the pan. Continue cooking, tossing often, until the beans are blistered in spots and become pliable, 4 to 6 minutes.

Add the walnuts, shallots, and garlic and stir well. Cover and continue to cook for 3 more minutes, shaking the pan occasionally. Add the ajika, tomato, and remaining 1½ teaspoons salt and cook, uncovered and stirring often, until the tomatoes break down and cling to the beans and the mixture smells aromatic, about 2 minutes. Add another splash of water to release any stuck-on bits from the bottom of the pan, if needed. Remove the pan from the heat and stir in the vinegar. Taste for seasoning and adjust to your liking. Pile the beans on a serving platter and garnish with lots of chopped cilantro.

FAVA BEAN PRIMAVERA WITH SPRING HAZELNUT–HERB PESTO

Makes 4 to 6 servings

As fava beans mature in spring, they are well protected from the chilly nights with a double layer: an exterior insulated pod and a waxy skin that surrounds the edible bean. These layers need to be shed to get to the tender legume within, and the extra work is certainly worth the effort. You'll be rewarded with this dish of sweet favas tossed with al dente pasta and a mixed-herb pesto—spring eating at its best.

¼ cup kosher salt

2 pounds fava bean pods

12 ounces tubular dried pasta, such as penne, ziti, or rigatoni

2 tablespoons extra virgin olive oil

1 bunch broccoli raab or broccolini, tough ends trimmed, cut into 1-inch pieces

1 recipe Spring Hazelnut–Herb Pesto (page 40)

½ lemon

Freshly grated Pecorino Romano cheese for garnish

Bring 3 quarts of water to a boil in a large pot over high heat and add the salt. Ready a large bowl of ice water.

Hold a fava bean pod in your hand with the stem end facing up. Snap off the tip toward one of the seams on either side of the bean and pull the string down the length of the bean. Pry open the pod at the seam to expose the beans. Collect the beans in a bowl and discard the husks. Repeat to shuck all of the beans from the pods.

Place the fava beans in the boiling water and cook for about 2 minutes, or until the water just reaches a rolling boil again. Use a slotted spoon to remove the beans from the water and drop them into the bowl of ice water to cool. Keep the pot of water on the stove for cooking the pasta.

When the fava beans are cooled, one at a time, tear the outer light green waxy shell of each bean and pinch out the bright green bean inside, discarding the shells.

Return the pot of water to a boil over high heat. Add the pasta, stir well, and cook until al dente according to the package directions. Reserve about 1 cup of the cooking water and drain the pasta in a colander.

In a wide skillet over medium heat, warm the oil until it shimmers. Add the broccoli raab and cook, stirring often, 2 to 3 minutes. Add the fava beans, cooked pasta, and enough pesto to coat the noodles and vegetables liberally (you may not need all the sauce, so save any extra for another use). Add just enough of the reserved cooking water to create a sauce that clings nicely to the noodles and vegetables. Finish with a squeeze of juice from the lemon half. Toss well and taste for seasoning and adjust to your liking. Tip the pasta onto a serving platter and shower with grated Pecorino.

WARM FIELD PEAS WITH TANGY PEPPER SAUCE

Makes 6 servings

Though these two recipes work harmoniously in concert together, I consider this my back-pocket recipe for slow-simmered field peas and use this technique often in a variety of ways. They are cooked simply with onions and celery to let the earthy peas take the lead. A tangy pureed pepper sauce provides a silky coating of acidity, sweetness, and heat, making this an elevated version of that classic duo of field peas and pepper sauce.

FIELD PEAS

2 tablespoons extra virgin olive oil

1 cup diced yellow onion

1 cup diced celery

1 tablespoon kosher salt

1/4 teaspoon freshly ground black pepper

1 1/2 pounds fresh shelled field peas, such as lady peas, black-eyed peas, pink-eyed peas, crowder peas, zipper peas, or a mix

1 tablespoon chopped flat-leaf parsley

TANGY PEPPER SAUCE

1/4 cup extra virgin olive oil

12 ounces sweet peppers (yellow, orange, red, or a mix)

1 small red onion, diced

1 jalapeño, seeded and chopped

3 cloves garlic, sliced

2 teaspoons kosher salt

3 tablespoons sherry vinegar

2 teaspoons fresh oregano leaves

TO COOK THE FIELD PEAS: In a medium saucepan, heat the oil over medium heat until it shimmers. Add the onions, celery, salt, and pepper. Decrease the heat to medium-low and cook, stirring occasionally, until tender, about 5 minutes. Add the shelled peas and 1 quart of water and bring to a gentle simmer. Cook until the peas are tender and creamy inside. Most varieties will take 30 to 40 minutes to cook, but begin checking them after 15 minutes, and then every 5 minutes or so until they are done.

TO MAKE THE PEPPER SAUCE: In a medium saucepan, warm the oil over medium heat. Add the sweet peppers, onions, jalapeño, garlic, and salt and cook until they are beginning to soften, 3 to 4 minutes. Cover, decrease the heat to medium-low, and continue to cook until the peppers are very tender, stirring occasionally, 12 to 15 minutes. Add the vinegar and oregano. Cover and cook 2 minutes more. Transfer the mixture to a blender and blend until velvety smooth. Taste for seasoning and adjust to your liking. (The sauce will keep in an airtight container in the refrigerator for up to 3 days. Reheat before serving.)

TO SERVE: Spread about 1/4 cup of the pepper sauce in the center of 6 salad plates or shallow bowls. Using a slotted spoon, divide the warm field peas over the sauce on each plate and garnish with the chopped parsley.

FRENCH LENTIL PICNIC SALAD

Makes 4 to 6 servings

I am a little obsessed with the notion of a picnic. It's that idea of packing up little presents of food to unwrap later in a pastoral setting and a super-fun way to simultaneously eat and appreciate companionship and nature. I cannot think of a better travel companion than this marinated French green lentil salad. I take care to finely dice the vegetables because I want them to be around the same size as the little lentils themselves. Notes of mustard, vinegar, and herbes de Provence lighten up this earthy legume and take it to a higher plane.

1½ cups French green lentils

1 head garlic

1 tablespoon kosher salt

1 cup finely diced carrots

1 cup finely diced celery

1 batch French Vinaigrette (page 18)

¼ cup chopped fresh flat-leaf parsley

2 tablespoons whole-grain mustard

1 teaspoon dried herbes de Provence

Place the lentils in a medium saucepan and cover them with 5 cups of water. Split the head of garlic in half crosswise through the widest part using a chef's knife and add the two halves to the pan. Set the pan over medium heat and bring to a lively simmer. Decrease the heat to maintain a gentle simmer, add the salt, and cook until the lentils are just tender but still hold their shape, 25 to 30 minutes.

Drain the cooked lentils in a colander and transfer them to a rimmed baking sheet to cool, stirring them occasionally to release the steam. Discard the garlic. While the lentils are still warm, add the carrots, celery, vinaigrette, parsley, mustard, and herbes de Provence. Let sit for at least 1 hour for the flavors to meld. Taste for seasoning and adjust to your liking. Serve the salad chilled or at room temperature. Any leftover salad will keep in an airtight container in the refrigerator for up to 3 days.

SPICY COCKTAIL MIX

Makes about 6 cups

Coconut, lime, chile, and fish sauce give this snack mix a zestier, bolder flavor than your average bagged version. The foundation of the mix is crispy field peas, which are first fried and then baked with a variety of crunchy bits and pieces you can purchase at most grocery stores. Feel free to swap out the suggested ones for any of your favorite simple crunchy snacks, nuts, and seeds to make it your own.

3 tablespoons coconut oil, melted

3 tablespoons fish sauce

2 teaspoons finely grated lime zest

1 teaspoon garlic powder

1 teaspoon onion powder

1 teaspoon freshly ground black pepper

1 teaspoon Thai or Korean chile powder

1 batch Crunchy Fried Field Peas or Beans (page 26)

1½ cups broken pretzel pieces

1 cup roasted cashews (see page 24)

1 cup sesame sticks

Heat the oven to 250°F with a rack in the middle.

In a large bowl, whisk the coconut oil, fish sauce, lime zest, garlic powder, onion powder, black pepper, and chile powder. Add the fried field peas or beans, pretzel pieces, cashews, and sesame sticks and mix well to coat everything evenly.

Spread the mixture on a large rimmed baking sheet and bake until the mixture is nicely browned and looks dry, about 1 hour, stirring once halfway through. Let cool completely before serving. The mixture will keep in an airtight container for up to 1 week.

GIGANTE BEANS WITH GREEK FLAVORS

Makes 6 to 8 servings

This recipe seems simple, but the creamy, sweet, and meaty texture of these giant beans and the deep flavor that develops as they slowly stew make it extra special. Don't skimp on the olive oil, and in place of dried Greek oregano, you can always use fresh. Serve a bowl of the beans in their sauce with good crusty bread and another drizzle of olive oil for a hearty lunch, or put the pot on the table as a side dish to a big Mediterranean-inspired meal.

1 pound dried gigante beans, large white lima beans, or corona beans

1/4 cup extra virgin olive oil, plus more for drizzling

1 cup diced yellow onion

2 cloves garlic, minced

1 tablespoon kosher salt

2 teaspoons dried Greek oregano

1/2 teaspoon crushed red pepper

1 tablespoon freshly squeezed lemon juice

Place the beans in a large bowl and cover them with 3 inches of water. Set aside at room temperature to soak for at least 6 hours or overnight, then drain.

In a Dutch oven, warm the oil over medium heat and add the onions, garlic, 1 teaspoon of the salt, the dried oregano, and crushed red pepper. Cook, stirring often, until the onions are translucent, about 5 minutes. Add the drained beans and just enough fresh water to cover them by 1/2 inch. Bring to a lively simmer then decrease the heat to maintain a gentle simmer. Cook the beans, uncovered, until very tender, about 1 hour. Skim the foam and any empty bean skins that rise to the surface. Make sure there is just enough liquid to cover the beans while they cook, adding more if needed.

Once the beans are tender, add the remaining 2 teaspoons of salt and the lemon juice and taste for seasoning. The beans should be very flavorful, earthy-sweet, a little tart, and well seasoned. Serve the beans with a little of the cooking liquid from the pot, and drizzle each portion with more olive oil.

GARBANZOS GUISADOS

Makes 6 to 8 servings

The Spanish word "guisado" means "stew" in English, and that's how the incredible flavor develops in this Puerto Rican–inspired chickpea dish. The chickpeas, or garbanzos, are stewed with bacon drippings, green olives, annatto, and a tangy sofrito. Make this the centerpiece of a quasi-vegetarian meal or serve it alongside grilled meats and your favorite slaw or salad. As with most slow-cooked bean dishes, I like to make this a day ahead to let the flavors intensify even more.

1 pound dried chickpeas

8 ounces thick-cut bacon, chopped

1 small red onion

2 cubanelle peppers, stemmed and seeded

1 head garlic, cloves separated and peeled

2 plum tomatoes

1/2 cup chopped green olives

1/4 cup extra virgin olive oil

2 tablespoons kosher salt

2 teaspoons ground annatto seed

1 teaspoon dried oregano

Place the chickpeas in a large bowl and cover them with 3 inches of water. Set aside at room temperature to soak for at least 6 hours or overnight, then drain.

In a Dutch oven over medium heat, cook the bacon until browned and crisp, stirring often, about 7 minutes. Add the drained chickpeas and just enough fresh water to cover them by 1/2 inch. Bring to a lively simmer, then decrease the heat to maintain a gentle simmer. Cover and cook until the chickpeas are quite tender, about 1 hour.

Meanwhile, make the sofrito. Very coarsely chop the red onion, cubanelle peppers, garlic, and plum tomatoes. Transfer the vegetables to a food processor and blitz to a coarse but uniform mixture.

Add the sofrito, green olives, oil, salt, annatto, and oregano to the cooked chickpeas. Increase the heat to bring it to a lively simmer, then decrease the heat to a gentle simmer and cook uncovered for 30 minutes. Taste for seasoning and adjust as needed.

CARROT AND CHICKPEA PANISSE

Makes 8 to 12 servings

Panisse is a rustic chickpea fritter from the South of France that is naturally gluten-free. It makes a particularly nice snack with an aperitif of rosé. Chickpea flour is simmered on the stove, much like polenta, and then chilled and set. It's then cut into thick batons that are pan-fried in olive oil until crisp and brown on the outside, while the interior is like a luscious savory custard. Here, carrots appear in two ways: freshly juiced and mixed with milk to make the batter, and the tops are used to make a Moroccan-spiced green sauce to spoon over the fritters. If you can't find carrots with tops, you can just use extra parsley and cilantro to replace them. And don't worry if you don't juice at home—store-bought pressed carrot juice is just fine.

Extra virgin olive oil, for greasing and frying

2 cups carrot juice (freshly juiced or store-bought)

2 cups whole milk

4 tablespoons unsalted butter

1 clove garlic, grated or pressed

1 tablespoon kosher salt

2 cups chickpea flour, sifted

1 recipe Carrot Top Chermoula (page 40), Salsa Verde (page 39), or Lemony Aioli (page 14)

Grease a 13-by-9-inch baking dish with oil and line the bottom with a sheet of parchment paper that hangs over each of the two longer sides of the dish like wings. Lightly grease the top of the parchment paper and set aside.

In a large saucepan, combine the carrot juice, milk, butter, garlic, and salt and bring to a simmer over medium heat. Whisk the chickpea flour vigorously into the warm milk mixture. (The mixture will at first look lumpy, but whisking will mostly smooth it out, and any remaining lumps will relax as the panisse sets.) Cook, stirring almost constantly with a wooden spoon, until the mixture becomes very thick and resembles a melty cheese sauce, about 10 minutes. Taste and add more salt, if needed.

Tip the mixture into the prepared baking dish. Lightly oil your hands and press it in an even layer all the way to the edges and corners of the pan, smoothing the surface to make it flat. The oil from your hands will also help prevent the mixture from forming a skin. Refrigerate, uncovered, until set, about 1 hour. (The dough can be made up to 2 days ahead.)

Lift the chilled panisse dough from the baking dish using the parchment wings and transfer it to a cutting board. Cut the dough lengthwise into thirds and then crosswise into batons that are about ¾ inch thick and 3 inches long.

Heat the oven to the lowest temperature or warming setting.

Heat a cast-iron skillet or other heavy frying pan over medium heat and add enough oil to lightly coat the bottom. When the oil shimmers, add about half of the panisse and fry until they are lightly browned and crisp, 2 to 3 minutes per side. Arrange the fried panisse on a platter and serve them immediately, or pop them into the warm oven while you repeat to fry another batch. Serve hot with the sauce of your choice.

NIGHTSHADES

Nightshades are a big, often misunderstood, plant family with a broad swath of varieties. The edible ones include tomatoes, potatoes, tomatillos, eggplant, sweet peppers, and hot chiles.

Tomatoes might be the most sought-after treasure at the summer produce stand. Beefsteak, cherry, roma, and a multitude of heirloom varieties seduce us with their colorful hues and interesting shapes. They are all alluring in their own way, with varying degrees of sweetness and acid, juiciness or pulpiness. Tomatillo, the little husk-wrapped green tomato from Mexico, is a tart and seedy fruit most commonly used for salsa verde.

Because potatoes are a staple in many cultures and the possibilities for their preparation are seemingly endless, there have been volumes written on them. Potatoes are chameleons in the kitchen—their versatile properties allow them to transform into a creamy gratin, crunchy fries, tender dumplings, or a fluffy mash.

Eggplant is the airy, spongy fruit of the nightshade family, and perhaps the most controversial. Because undercooked eggplant has a chalky, unpleasant texture, it is important to break down those spongy cell walls until they give in to the heat. I've highlighted two lesser-known techniques for cooking eggplant: coal-roasting them whole, and brining then frying them into crispy wedges, which both yield soft, creamy flesh inside.

The underripe green bell pepper has a vegetal taste, but let it sit on the vine and it will ripen, become sweeter, and change to its predetermined color of yellow, orange, red, or even purple. There are many types of peppers besides the common bell, from little Italian fryers to pimento to padron and shishito. The smaller ones can be blistered in a hot skillet, larger ones can be grilled whole or fire roasted, and all of them are suitable for slicing, dicing, or pureeing into a silky sweet sauce.

Hot chiles have varying degrees of heat produced by capsaicin, which is found mostly in their ribs and seeds, so you can adjust the spice level by removing these parts. There is a world of condiments dedicated to hot chiles. In their dried form, they are used as a spice when ground, or as a flavor base for salsas, sauces, and stews.

CHERRY TOMATO CROSTATA

Makes 6 servings

Tomato tart is a summertime favorite. Cherry tomatoes work well because they give off less water and keep the crust crisp, while tomato jam brings a concentrated tomato layer at the base of the tart and absorbs those bubbling tomato juices as it bakes. A drizzle of honey heightens the sweetness.

DOUGH

1 1/4 cup unbleached all-purpose flour, plus more for dusting

1/2 cup fine semolina flour

1 teaspoon fine sea salt

3/4 cup (1 1/2 sticks) unsalted butter, cubed and chilled

1/3 cup ice-cold water

FILLING

1 heaping pint cherry tomatoes, stemmed and halved, or quartered if large

2 tablespoons honey, plus more for drizzling

2 tablespoons extra virgin olive oil

1 teaspoon fresh thyme leaves

1 1/2 teaspoons kosher salt

1/8 teaspoon freshly ground black pepper

1/2 cup Spiced Tomato Jam (page 34)

1 egg

Flaky sea salt

TO MAKE THE DOUGH: Whisk both flours and the salt in a medium mixing bowl. Add the cold butter and toss with your hands to coat it in the flour. Smear the butter between your fingers to make small streaks the size of peas. Add the cold water and stir just to combine and moisten the flour, being careful not to overwork the dough. When the dough just comes together, transfer the mixture to a clean surface dusted with flour. Flatten the dough out with the palms of your hands, then roll it out about 1/2 inch thick using a floured rolling pin. Fold the dough over on itself twice and repeat rolling it out and folding it 3 times to create layers, which will lead to a flaky crust. After the last fold, press the dough into a flat disk and wrap it tightly with plastic film. Refrigerate for at least 1 hour and up to 2 days before using.

TO MAKE THE FILLING: In a medium bowl, combine the cherry tomatoes, honey, oil, thyme, salt, and pepper and mix well. Let this mixture sit out at room temperature to macerate for 15 minutes or up to 1 hour. Drain the juices into a small pan and bring to a simmer over medium heat. Simmer until it thickens to coat the back of a spoon, 4 to 6 minutes. Let the syrup cool briefly then add it back to the tomatoes.

Line a large rimmed baking sheet with a sheet of parchment paper and set aside. Pull the dough from the refrigerator and place it on a floured surface. Using a floured rolling pin, roll the dough out to a 15-inch circle, rotating it occasionally to be sure it isn't sticking, and dusting with additional flour as needed. Spread the tomato jam in the center of the cold dough, leaving a 2-inch naked edge. Spread the cherry tomato mixture over the jam in an even layer. Fold the edges of dough over the filling, overlapping every 4 inches to create an evenly pleated crust. Refrigerate until well chilled before baking, about 20 minutes.

Heat the oven to 375°F with a rack in the center position. In a small bowl, beat the egg with 2 teaspoons of water. Remove the crostata from the refrigerator and brush the egg wash on the crust. Bake until the crust is lightly browned and the tomato filling is hot and bubbly, 40 to 45 minutes. Let cool for 10 to 15 minutes.

Drizzle the entire crostata with honey and sprinkle some flaky sea salt over the top, especially on the crust. Serve warm or at room temperature.

HEIRLOOM TOMATO AND PEACH JUICE

Makes 2 servings; about 2 3/4 cups

Many varieties of heirloom tomatoes have extra-juicy flesh, and when they become too ripe for slicing, they can feel heavy and soft to the touch. That's when I like to turn them into fresh tomato juice, blended with other summer fruits. A ripe peach is the perfect complement, along with a little fresh ginger, lemon, and some sea salt. Make sure the juice is well chilled for my version of summer in a glass.

2 cold heirloom tomatoes (about 1 pound), quartered and cored

One (1-inch) piece fresh ginger, peeled

2 cold peaches (about 1 pound), halved and pitted

1/4 cup fresh lemon juice, chilled

1/2 teaspoon fine sea salt, plus more as needed

Process the tomatoes, ginger, and peaches through a juicer, in that order. Alternatively, you can process the ingredients together in a blender on high speed until smooth. If using a blender, or if the juice has more pulp than desired, strain it through a fine-mesh sieve. Stir in the lemon juice and salt and serve chilled.

GREEN TOMATO AND SWEET ONION RELISH

Makes 2 cups

In the South, there are so many variations of green tomato relish, because it's a tried-and-true way of using those underripe tomatoes left clinging to the vine at the end of the season. But many of them I find too sweet and a little one-note. Fresh herbal flavors give it an update, with the mild tang of white balsamic vinegar and the subtle sweetness of anise and fennel. Serve it with charcuterie, as a condiment at a summer cookout, or with fresh cheeses.

1½ pounds green tomatoes, diced

1 large sweet onion, such as Vidalia or Walla Walla, diced

1 cup white balsamic vinegar

¼ cup honey

2 teaspoons kosher salt

1 teaspoon celery seeds

1 teaspoon anise or fennel seeds

2 teaspoons chopped fresh dill

2 teaspoons chopped fennel fronds (optional)

Combine the green tomatoes, onions, vinegar, honey, salt, celery seeds, and anise or fennel seeds in a medium saucepan. Place the pan over medium heat and bring the liquid to a lively simmer. Adjust the heat to maintain a gentle simmer and cook until the relish is thickened, about 1 hour, stirring often to avoid scorching on the bottom of the pan. The relish will continue to thicken as it cools, so remove it from the heat when it is a little looser than a chunky marmalade. Allow it to cool to room temperature.

Once cooled, stir in the dill and fennel fronds, if using. Chill until ready to serve or store it in an airtight container in the refrigerator for up to 1 week.

BEEFSTEAK BLT SALAD

Makes 4 servings

This is everything you love about a BLT sandwich in a bowl. It's just as easy to pull together this vegetable-forward version, and the sum is greater than the parts. Because there are few ingredients, make sure they are all top quality. Chop a peak-season tomato and a head of tender lettuce. Fry up the bacon and make some really good croutons—both done in the oven. You can use store-bought mayonnaise in a pinch, but homemade is easy to blitz together while you wait.

8 slices thick-cut bacon

4 slices stale bread, cubed (about 5 cups)

1 tablespoon unsalted butter, melted

2 beefsteak tomatoes, diced

½ teaspoon kosher salt

½ teaspoon freshly ground black pepper

2 tablespoons Homemade Mayonnaise (page 14), or store-bought is fine

1½ tablespoons fresh lemon juice

1 large head of lettuce such as red butter, green bibb, baby romaine, or a mix

Heat the oven to 350°F.

Place the bacon slices on a rimmed baking sheet and bake until it's mostly crispy, but still a little meaty and fatty in some parts, 15 to 20 minutes. Once the bacon is ready, transfer the cooked slices to a plate lined with paper towels and reserve the pan with the bacon fat. When cool, cut the bacon into bite-size pieces.

Meanwhile, in a medium bowl, toss the bread cubes with the melted butter to coat. Add the bread cubes to the baking sheet and toss in the bacon fat until well coated. Bake until just crisp and golden brown but still a little chewy in the middle, 10 to 15 minutes.

Place the diced tomatoes in a large mixing bowl. Season them with the salt and pepper, then add the mayonnaise and lemon juice. Stir well to combine. The juices from the tomatoes will mix with the mayonnaise and lemon to make a pink-colored creamy tomato dressing.

Trim the base from each head of lettuce and wash the leaves well, then dry them in a salad spinner. Tear or cut the leaves into bite-size pieces and add them to the bowl with the tomato dressing. Add the croutons and bacon and toss well to combine. Taste for seasoning and adjust to your liking.

TOMATILLO CHICKEN

Makes 8 to 10 servings

Tomatillos have a rather tart flavor, and they're high in pectin, which gives body, making them ideal for sauces and salsa. Roasting brings out their savory-sweet side. This dish begins by making a roasted tomatillo salsa that, by the way, is great on its own as a condiment. But take it a step further and use it to braise chicken to feed a crowd. Serve the pulled chicken from the pot with warm tortillas and lots of toppings, like sour cream, cilantro, radishes, and pickled jalapeños. It also makes an outstanding filling for enchiladas, or better yet, a cheesy layered tortilla casserole. Leftovers make a fabulous filling for my Poblano Chiles Rellenos on page 238.

1 pound tomatillos

½ white onion, cut into ½-inch-thick wedges

1 poblano, stemmed, halved lengthwise, and seeded

1 to 2 jalapeño chiles (1 for mild, 2 for spicier)

3 cloves garlic (unpeeled)

3 tablespoons extra virgin olive oil

1 tablespoon kosher salt

¾ cup coarsely chopped cilantro leaves and stems

1 teaspoon ground cumin

3 pounds boneless, skinless chicken thighs

Heat the broiler to high with a rack positioned 6 to 8 inches below. Remove the papery husks from the tomatillos and scrub them under running water to remove the sticky residue.

Pile the whole tomatillos, onion wedges, poblano halves, whole jalapeños, and garlic cloves in the center of a large rimmed baking sheet. Drizzle with 1 tablespoon of the oil and sprinkle with 1 teaspoon of the salt. Spread it all out in a single layer.

Broil until everything is blistered and lightly charred, about 20 minutes. Turn everything except the onions when they are done on the first side, about halfway through the cooking time. Remove each ingredient as it's done and set aside to cool. The onions will take the longest to char, so just get them nicely browned on one side.

When cool enough to handle, squeeze the garlic cloves from their charred skins and discard the skins. Peel any loose charred bits of skin from the chiles (but it's okay to leave them on if you'd like) and stem the jalapeños. Put the charred ingredients (tomatillos, onions, chiles, garlic cloves, and any accumulated juices) in a blender and add the cilantro, cumin, and 1 cup of water. Blend on high to get a relatively smooth salsa.

In a large Dutch oven, heat the remaining 2 tablespoons of oil over medium-high heat until it shimmers. Season the chicken on both sides with the remaining 2 teaspoons of salt. Working in batches, sear the chicken thighs on both sides in the hot oil, adding just enough to avoid overcrowding the pan, about 5 minutes per side. After searing the final batch, return all the chicken thighs back to the pan along with any accumulated juices. Pour in the salsa and bring to a simmer. Cover and braise at a gentle simmer until the chicken is very tender and shreds easily, about 1 hour. Turn off the heat and use two forks to pull the chicken apart. Stir the chicken into the sauce and taste for seasoning and adjust to your liking.

COAL-ROASTED EGGPLANT DIP

Makes 6 to 8 servings; about 2¼ cups

When I build a fire for grilling, I like to cook several things so the effort is not in vain. But the cooking does not all have to happen on top of the grill grates. While you still have hot coals, use this technique for burying a whole eggplant in the remaining embers. This creamy dip is similar to baba ghanoush, but it's made with sunflower butter instead of sesame tahini. Serve the dip as the centerpiece of a mezze platter with fresh vegetables, grilled pita, and good-quality feta.

2 globe eggplants (about 1¾ pounds)

¼ cup sunflower butter (see Note)

¼ cup fresh lemon juice

1 clove garlic, minced

2 teaspoons smoked sea salt or medium-grain plain sea salt, plus more for garnish

Smoked paprika for garnish

Prepare a hot fire in a charcoal grill and let the coals die down until the embers are glowing. Push aside some of the hot embers so you have a thin base layer in the center of the grill. Place the eggplants over this base layer and shovel the remaining embers over and around each one to partially cover them. Let the eggplants roast in the embers until the skin is completely charred and wrinkly and they look deflated, turning once, about 18 to 20 minutes. Set the eggplants aside until cool enough to handle.

Remove the stem end and most of the charred skin from each eggplant with your hands, but it's okay if some small bits of char are still clinging to the flesh. Place the eggplant in a food processor and add the sunflower butter, lemon juice, garlic, and salt. Puree until smooth, about 1 minute, scraping down the sides as needed.

Spoon the dip into a serving bowl and sprinkle with smoked paprika and a little more salt.

NOTE: Try to get sunflower butter (or "sun butter") that is just made of roasted sunflower seeds, without added ingredients like sugar.

BRINED EGGPLANT FRITES WITH HARISSA

Makes 6 to 8 servings

I prefer Chinese or Japanese eggplants for this recipe, because they have a long, slender shape that is easy to trim into thick-cut fries. But if you cannot find them, globe eggplants work just fine too. The most important factor is the saltwater brining method. Eggplants are like sponges, and they actually have tiny air pockets between their cells, so they drink up any moisture that they come into contact with. Soaking them in the brine infuses the flesh with moisture and seasoning, so when they're fried in the hot oil, you get a very tender center with super-crispy edges from the cornstarch coating. My pepper harissa sauce adds just the right amount of sweetness, spice, and tang for dipping.

½ cup kosher salt

1½ pounds Chinese or Japanese eggplant

1 cup cornstarch

About 3 cups canola oil for frying

Flaky sea salt for finishing

Piment d'Espelette (see Note on page 122) for garnish

Coarsely chopped parsley for garnish

1 recipe Sweet Pepper Harissa (page 33)

Place the salt in a 6-quart container (like a stockpot) and add 1 gallon of water. Stir vigorously until the salt is dissolved and set aside.

Trim the top from each eggplant and peel the skins using a vegetable peeler. Cut the eggplant flesh into wedges that are about 1 inch thick and 3 to 4 inches long, like hand-cut steak fries. Place the eggplant wedges in the saltwater brine. Place a few plates on top of the eggplant to weigh them down, keeping them submerged. Allow the eggplant to sit in the brine for 1 to 2 hours, then drain the eggplant in a colander.

Place the cornstarch in a large bowl. Add the brined eggplant wedges and toss to coat them evenly. Transfer the eggplant to a baking sheet, shaking off excess cornstarch. Line a second baking sheet with paper towels and set it near the stove.

Fill a cast-iron skillet or other wide, heavy frying pan with enough oil to come about ½ inch up the side of the pan and place it over medium heat. Position a thermometer in the oil, and begin frying when it reaches 325°F. Gently place about one-third of the eggplant wedges in the oil, or enough to fit in a single layer without crowding the pan. Cook until the wedges are light golden brown and crisp on each side, 5 to 7 minutes, turning each piece over once halfway through. Adjust the heat as needed to maintain the oil temperature throughout frying. Using tongs or a slotted spoon, remove the eggplant wedges from the oil and transfer them to the baking sheet lined with paper towels. While still hot, season with flaky sea salt and piment d'Espelette. Repeat to fry the remaining eggplant.

Sprinkle the eggplant fries with parsley and serve them while they're hot, with the harissa for dipping.

CRISPY GOLDEN NEW POTATOES WITH COCONUT–CILANTRO CHUTNEY

Makes 4 to 6 servings

New potatoes have a waxy texture that benefits from a twice-cooked technique. The potatoes are first simmered in a flavorful stock to tenderize the flesh. Then I tear the potatoes into craggy, uneven pieces and pan-fry them—all those nooks and crannies create more surface area for maximum crispiness. The contrast of creamy interior and crispy exterior is my holy grail of potato cookery. Inspiration for this dish comes from masala dosas, those Indian crepes that are filled with spiced potatoes and served with chutney, and I make this when I'm craving those flavors.

2 pounds new potatoes

3/4 cup kosher salt, plus more

3/4 cup distilled vinegar

3 tablespoons ground turmeric

1 tablespoon black peppercorns

3 bay leaves

3/4 cup coconut oil

1 handful toasted coconut flakes (see page 24)

1 handful cilantro leaves

1 recipe Quick Coconut-Cilantro Chutney (page 31)

Place the potatoes in a 6-quart Dutch oven and cover them with 3 quarts of cold water. Add the salt, vinegar, turmeric, peppercorns, and bay leaves and bring to a simmer over medium-high heat. Adjust the heat to maintain a gentle simmer and cook until the potatoes are fork tender and their skins begin to crack, 30 to 45 minutes. Drain the potatoes in a colander and set aside until they are cool enough to handle. Using your hands, tear the warm potatoes into halves or large bite-size pieces.

In a 12-inch skillet, heat the coconut oil over medium-high heat. Place the potato pieces torn side down in the hot oil and cook, undisturbed, until deeply browned and crispy, 10 to 15 minutes. If they begin to brown too fast, decrease the heat a little. The goal is to slowly cook them in the hot oil to allow them to get really crisp without burning. Turn the potatoes over and brown them on the other side, about 10 minutes. Remove the potatoes from the pan with a slotted spoon or spatula and place them on a tray lined with paper towels. Season with a little more salt while they are piping hot, then pile the potatoes on a serving platter and garnish with coconut and cilantro. Serve with the chutney on the side.

YUKON GOLD TARTIFLETTE

Makes 6 to 8 servings

Tartiflette is a rich French potato gratin that hails from the Alpine region of Savoie. It's a hearty, comforting dish served après-ski with a bottle of the region's minerally white wines. My version borrows from neighboring Italy, with funky taleggio cheese and meaty bits of pancetta in the mix. This is undoubtedly a decadent cold-weather dish, and worth the splurge. Serve it with a tender green salad dressed in a tart vinaigrette for balance.

8 ounces pancetta, diced

1 large leek, trimmed, sliced, and washed well (see page 70)

1 cup dry white wine

1 tablespoon fresh thyme leaves

2 teaspoons kosher salt

1 teaspoon freshly ground black pepper

3 pounds Yukon Gold potatoes

8 ounces taleggio cheese, rinds trimmed, cut into small chunks

1 cup heavy cream

Heat the oven to 375°F with a rack in the center.

Combine the pancetta and ½ cup water in a medium skillet and place it over medium heat. Cook, stirring occasionally, until the water has evaporated and the pancetta is lightly browned, 10 to 12 minutes. Remove the pancetta with a slotted spoon and transfer it to a small bowl, leaving the fat in the pan. Decrease the heat to medium-low and add the leek to the pan. Cook until tender and lightly browned, 5 to 7 minutes. Add the wine, thyme, ½ teaspoon of the salt, and ¼ teaspoon of the pepper. Bring to a simmer, scraping up the bits from the bottom of the pan. Remove the pan from the heat and set aside.

Using a mandoline with a hand guard, cut the unpeeled potatoes into ⅛-inch-thick slices. Alternatively, you can cut the potatoes in half lengthwise with a chef's knife, place them cut side down on the cutting board, and thinly slice.

In a 2½- to 3-quart baking dish, overlap about one-third of the potato slices to cover the bottom of the dish in an even layer. Season the potatoes with ½ teaspoon of the salt and ¼ teaspoon of the pepper. Using a slotted spoon, remove about half of the leeks from the wine mixture and scatter them over the top of the potatoes, then sprinkle with half of the pancetta. Repeat to make another layer using one-third of the potatoes seasoned with ½ teaspoon of the salt and ¼ teaspoon of the pepper, the remaining half of the leeks strained from the wine mixture, and the remaining pancetta. Add a final layer, using up the remaining potatoes, salt, and pepper. Scatter the taleggio over the potatoes. Drizzle the wine mixture evenly over the top, followed by the cream, coating the entire surface.

Place the baking dish on a large rimmed baking sheet and bake until the potatoes are tender, the sauce is bubbling, and the top is lightly browned, 60 to 80 minutes. Let the tartiflette rest for 15 minutes before serving.

GARLICKY TWICE-BAKED POTATOES WITH MUSHROOMS AND KALE

Makes 4 servings

Who doesn't love a twice-baked potato? But it's time for an update on this old-school side. My goal here was to make them slightly less decadent, but every bit as delicious. This modern take uses kefir, which is fermented milk that has the tang of yogurt in a pourable consistency (but you could substitute buttermilk if you like). Instead of shredded cheese, I opt for a shredded kale salad and some roasted mushrooms piled on top to make it a complete meal.

4 russet potatoes, scrubbed

1 recipe Garlic Confit and Garlic Oil (page 30), separated

1 tablespoon plus 2¾ teaspoons kosher salt

4 ounces oyster mushrooms, torn into bite-size pieces

½ teaspoon freshly ground black pepper

4 tablespoons unsalted butter, at room temperature

1½ cups plain kefir or buttermilk

2 cups thinly sliced lacinato kale

4 green onions, thinly sliced

2 teaspoons fresh lemon juice

Heat the oven to 400°F. Place the potatoes in a baking dish with space between them. Poke each potato all over with the tines of a fork. Rub them with 2 teaspoons of the garlic oil to lightly coat and season on all sides with 1 tablespoon of the salt. Roast the potatoes until very tender, 60 to 75 minutes.

In a medium bowl, toss the oyster mushrooms with 1 tablespoon of the garlic oil and season with ½ teaspoon of the salt and ¼ teaspoon of the pepper. Spread the mushrooms on a rimmed baking sheet in an even layer. Roast on the upper oven rack until the edges are crispy and lightly browned, 10 to 15 minutes.

While the potatoes are still warm but just cool enough to handle, cut a deep slit lengthwise across the top of each, and another slit crosswise. Using both hands, gently push at the base of each potato, applying pressure with your fingertips to break up the flesh and release steam. Gently scoop out as much flesh as you can while keeping the potato skin intact and transfer the flesh to the bowl of a stand mixer or other large bowl.

Mash the garlic confit into a paste and add it to the bowl of potatoes. Add the butter, 2 teaspoons of the salt, and the remaining ¼ teaspoon pepper. Using the stand mixer fitted with the whisk attachment, or a handheld electric mixer, whip the potatoes on medium-low speed until well mixed. With the motor running, add the kefir and whip until the potatoes are light and fluffy.

Spoon the whipped potatoes back into the skins, piling some up and out of the top. Return the potatoes to the oven to warm through, 10 to 15 minutes.

In a small bowl, toss the kale, green onions, lemon juice, 1 tablespoon of garlic oil, and ¼ teaspoon of salt.

Top the hot potatoes with the mushrooms and the kale salad, letting excess fall onto the plate to scoop up with each bite.

BELL PEPPER GRAVY SHRIMP AND GRITS

Makes 4 servings

There's a period in late summer when it's too damn hot in Georgia for tomatoes to grow, but peppers are beginning to flourish. It was during this time when I came up with this idea for a new twist on a Southern classic. Shrimp and grits is historically made with a tomato-studded sauce, but because we had so many peppers on hand, I worked them into the recipe in two ways. They replace the tomato in the shrimp sauté, and also get blended into a velvety sweet pepper sauce that coats every bite.

GRITS

3 cups whole milk

1½ cups corn grits or polenta

3 tablespoons unsalted butter

1 tablespoon kosher salt

½ teaspoon freshly ground black pepper

½ teaspoon lemon zest

BELL PEPPER GRAVY

2 tablespoons unsalted butter

½ yellow onion, diced

2 red or yellow bell peppers, seeds and ribs removed, diced

1 jalapeño or serrano chile, diced

1 clove garlic, sliced

2 teaspoons kosher salt

1 teaspoon fresh oregano leaves

½ cup buttermilk

SHRIMP

4 tablespoons unsalted butter

½ yellow onion, halved and sliced into thin, crescent-shaped wedges

1 red or yellow bell pepper, seeds and ribs removed, cut into thin strips

1½ teaspoons kosher salt

1½ pounds large shrimp, peeled and deveined

1 teaspoon sweet paprika

Juice of one lemon

TO MAKE THE GRITS: In a medium saucepan, combine the milk with 3 cups of water and place it over medium heat. When the mixture just begins to steam, whisk in the grits, butter, and salt until smooth. Turn the heat down to low and continue to cook, stirring often, until the grits thicken and tenderize, about 20 minutes. Stir in the pepper and lemon zest. Taste for seasoning and adjust as desired. Turn off the heat and cover the pan with a lid to keep warm until you're ready to serve.

TO MAKE THE GRAVY: Melt the butter in a wide skillet over medium heat. Add the onions, bell pepper, chile, garlic, salt, and oregano. Cook until the onions are translucent and the peppers are tender, 6 to 8 minutes. Add the buttermilk and continue to cook for 1 more minute (it may curdle but it will not affect the outcome). Transfer the mixture to a blender and blend on high speed until smooth, about 1 minute. Taste for seasoning and adjust to your liking.

TO COOK THE SHRIMP: Melt the butter in a wide skillet over medium heat. Add the onions and pepper and season with ½ teaspoon of the salt. Cook, stirring often, until the onions and peppers are almost tender, about 5 minutes. Add the shrimp, paprika, lemon juice, and remaining 1 teaspoon of salt. Cook, stirring occasionally, until the shrimp turn pink and begin to curl, 3 to 4 minutes. Remove the pan from the heat.

TO SERVE: Divide the warm grits among shallow dinner bowls. Spoon some of the gravy over the grits, then top with the shrimp mixture. Add a little more gravy to each serving.

PEPERONATA

Makes about 1 quart

Make this when you come across sweet Italian frying peppers, especially my favorite, the horn-shaped corno di toro variety, at the market. Because of their slender, tapered shape, they are easy to cut into uniform rings for this simple relish that's the ideal accompaniment to so many things. Of course, they are a staple on an antipasti platter, but I also like them layered into an Italian-style sandwich, as a topping for a mixed salad, or spooned over any roasted vegetables for a little kick. For even more kick, throw some hot banana peppers into the mix.

2 cups apple cider vinegar

2 tablespoons kosher salt

1/3 cup honey

1 cup extra virgin olive oil

2 pounds Italian frying peppers, thinly sliced

1 red onion, halved and thinly sliced

3 cloves garlic, thinly sliced

In a large bowl, whisk the vinegar, salt, and honey with 2½ cups of water and set aside.

In a medium skillet, heat the oil over medium-low heat until it shimmers. Carefully drop a few handfuls of the peppers, onions, and garlic into the hot oil and gently fry until the vegetables are crisp-tender, 2 to 3 minutes. Using a slotted spoon, strain the fried vegetables from the oil and transfer them to the bowl with the vinegar mixture. Repeat to fry the remaining peppers, onions, and garlic in batches, and add them to the vinegar mixture. Let the oil cool and then add it to the bowl too.

Serve the peperonata at room temperature. It will keep in an airtight container in the refrigerator for up to 1 month.

POBLANO CHILES RELLENOS

Makes 6 servings

Although I've been enjoying chiles rellenos at my favorite Mexican restaurants for years, I never understood how they were made until a friend showed me the process a few years ago. Now I'm hooked. Fire-roasted poblano chiles are stuffed and coated in fluffy beaten eggs and pan-fried to get that unique exterior. It's essentially an omelet-coated stuffed pepper. The filling is dealer's choice. Traditionally it's stringy Oaxacan cheese that is akin to mozzarella and melts beautifully. But they can also be filled with potatoes, spiced ground beef, or my Tomatillo Chicken (page 220). Whatever you choose, just make sure the filling is well seasoned, fully cooked, and cooled before stuffing the peppers. I like to serve them as a meal over saucy black beans and topped with salsa and fresh cilantro, but they also make a tasty snack on their own.

6 large poblano chiles

3 cups cold filling, such as shredded Oaxacan cheese, cooked potatoes, spiced ground beef, or shredded chicken

5 eggs

½ teaspoon kosher salt

⅔ cup all-purpose flour

1 cup canola oil

If you have a gas range, turn two burners on high heat and set two chiles on each burner over the open flames. Cook until the skins are charred black on all sides, using tongs to turn them occasionally, 2 to 3 minutes per side. Alternatively, you can broil the chiles. Position an oven rack about 6 to 8 inches below the heating element and turn the broiler to high. Place the chiles on a baking sheet and broil until the skins are evenly charred, turning occasionally, 15 to 20 minutes. Remove the chiles when they are done and place them in a large bowl. Cover with plastic film and let sit for about 10 minutes to steam the skins free.

Heat the oven to 275ºF.

Using your fingers or a paring knife, pull or scrape away the blistered skins from the chiles, being careful to keep them whole. Wear a pair of disposable gloves while doing this, if you have some handy. You may need to use a towel to brush away some of the charred bits of skin. Cut a slit on a flat side of each chile and stuff with about ½ cup of the filling of your choice. You want them to be nicely stuffed, but the slits should still be able to close.

Crack the eggs and separate the yolks and whites, placing the yolks in a small bowl and the whites in the bowl of a stand mixer or other large bowl. Add the salt to the egg whites. Using the stand mixer fitted with the whisk attachment, or a handheld electric mixer, beat the egg whites until glossy stiff peaks form. Stir the egg yolks with a fork until they are smooth. Using a spatula, fold the yolks into the whites and set the bowl near the stove.

Place the flour in a shallow dish. One at a time, roll each stuffed chile in the flour to coat the outside evenly and set them on a platter near the stove.

In a 12-inch nonstick or cast-iron skillet, heat ⅓ cup of the oil over medium high heat. As the oil is heating, hold a chile by the stem and dip it into the egg mixture, swirling it around until it's thoroughly coated in a thick layer. You may need to use your other hand to help spread the egg mixture evenly across the surface of the chile. Take note of which side the slit is on and place the coated chile slit

Continue to page 239 for the rest of the recipe

side down in the hot oil. (This helps make a seal so that the filling doesn't leak out.) Repeat to coat 2 more of the chiles and add them to the pan. Cook until the egg coating is browned and set on the bottom, 3 to 4 minutes. Using a slotted spatula, flip the chile over to cook on the other side, 2 to 3 minutes more. If there is still some raw egg coating on areas that didn't make contact with the hot oil, just turn the chile a quarter turn and cook a moment longer. Transfer the chiles to a rimmed baking sheet as they are done. Add the remaining ⅓ cup of oil to the pan, and repeat to fry the remaining 3 chiles, then add them to the baking sheet.

Place the chiles in the oven and bake until the interior is heated through and registers about 150ºF or higher on an instant-read thermometer, 15 to 20 minutes. Serve the chiles hot from the oven.

BLISTERED PARTY PEPPERS

Makes 4 to 6 servings

It happens every time—friends show up for dinner and the group naturally migrates to the kitchen. After everyone has a drink in hand, it's fun to make a live-action appetizer. The sizzle of the pan matches the buzz in the room. It's fun, it's fast, and everyone is wowed by the flavor of these petite peppers served over a zippy sauce.

1 tablespoon canola oil

8 ounces shishito or padron peppers

½ teaspoon kosher salt

Juice of half of a lime

1 recipe Lime Tahini Sauce (page 38), Pistachio Romesco (page 42), or Chipotle Mayo (page 14)

⅓ cup crumbled goat's milk feta cheese

2 teaspoons toasted sesame seeds

¼ cup coarsely chopped cilantro

In a wide cast-iron skillet, heat the oil over medium-high heat until it shimmers. Add the peppers to the pan and season with salt, then turn the heat up to high. Immediately place a lid over the pan to avoid oil splatters and to trap in the heat, and let the peppers cook undisturbed for 1 minute. Shake the pan vigorously while holding the lid, then cook 2 to 3 minutes more, shaking occasionally, until the peppers are blistered in spots. Remove the pan from the heat and turn any peppers over that have only browned on one side. Return the pan to the heat, cover, and cook until the peppers are tender and evenly blistered, 1 to 2 minutes more. Add a squeeze of lime, cover, and shake the pan really well one more time while holding the lid in place, then remove the pan from the heat.

Spread the tahini sauce across 4 individual plates or a serving platter and arrange the cooked peppers on top. Garnish with the crumbled feta, sesame seeds, and cilantro and serve immediately.

CUCURBITS

The botanical family of cucurbits—which includes cucumbers, watermelons, musk melons, pumpkins, and squash—are all technically fruit, though some are culinarily treated as vegetables.

Fall squash varieties are cured and dried to improve their sweetness, which makes them shelf-stable and in season during the autumn and winter months. There are so many varieties, each possessing surprisingly unique flavor, texture, and sweetness, that different cooking techniques truly highlight the best qualities each has to offer. The creamy, cup-shaped acorn squash is perfect for stuffing, and the cylindrical delicata can be sliced into rings, while the natural strands of spaghetti squash mimic angel hair pasta. Let's not forget the squash seeds, a versatile ingredient often discarded—use them for a crunchy topping or blended into a creamy broth.

In terms of flexibility, summer squash are limber vegetables: their textures can be expressed in so many ways, and their mild flavor is ideal for soaking up bold sauces. Think about thick slices of zucchini charred on the grill, or petite pattypan squash gently steamed. And although summer squash are most commonly expressed in savory ways, they can be used in sweet applications too.

The cool cucumber is found in diverse cultural cuisines, and has as many preparations. They can be smashed with fish sauce and lime, infused into a refreshing libation, and even marinated and grilled—they are surprisingly delicious when cooked, softening their crunch into a meaty texture and introducing layers of umami.

Cutting open a perfectly ripe, juicy melon and taking that first bite is a familiar pleasure, but when enhanced by salt, fat, or acid it becomes an extra special treat. Blend melons into chilled soups and frozen drinks, add them to salads, and serve them as a poolside snack or refreshing dessert.

ROASTED DELICATA WITH SQUASH SEED DUKKAH

Makes 4 to 6 servings

Dukkah is an Egyptian all-purpose condiment traditionally composed of hazelnuts or pistachios mixed with sesame seeds and spices, and each native household has its own family version. In an attempt to remain authentic to my region, I emulate dukkah using roasted squash seeds mixed with heirloom sesame seeds and Georgia peanuts. The result is completely addictive. I first tried roasting sweet delicata squash in peanut oil when I was working on recipes for my cookbook *Peanuts*, and found it brings out its earthy flavor. Unlike most fall squash, delicata has a very thin, edible skin, so there's no need to peel away its ridged exterior.

2 medium or 3 small delicata squash (about 2 pounds)

¼ cup plus 1 tablespoon peanut oil

2 teaspoons kosher salt

½ cup toasted sesame seeds

½ cup unsalted roasted peanuts

1 tablespoon ground coriander

1 tablespoon ground cumin

1 tablespoon freshly ground black pepper

Sliced fresh mint leaves for garnish

Heat the oven to 375°F with racks in the upper and lower thirds. Line two large rimmed baking sheets with parchment paper or silicone baking mats.

Wash the squash well and rub the skin vigorously to remove any traces of dirt in the crevices. Using a heavy knife, cut each squash in half crosswise. Use a spoon to scrape and dig out the seeds and surrounding stringy flesh into a medium bowl and set aside.

Slice the squash into ½-inch-thick rings. Place the rings in a large bowl and toss them with 3 tablespoons of the oil and 1 teaspoon of the salt. Spread the squash rings in a single layer on one of the prepared baking sheets.

In the same bowl, toss the seeds and stringy bits with the remaining 2 tablespoons of oil. Transfer the seeds to the other baking sheet and press down firmly to loosen the clusters and break apart the fibers, spreading them into a single, flat layer.

Place the squash rings on the lower rack of the oven, and the seeds on the upper rack. Roast until the seeds are toasted and brittle and the surrounding flesh is dried and browned, being careful not to let them burn, 12 to 17 minutes, stirring once halfway through. Roast the squash rings without turning them until tender and nicely browned on the bottom, 20 to 25 minutes. Remove both pans from the oven and let cool.

Meanwhile, to make the dukkah, combine the cooled squash seeds, sesame seeds, peanuts, coriander, cumin, black pepper, and remaining 1 teaspoon salt in a food processor, and pulverize until it is a coarse, uniform mixture. Transfer the dukkah to a shallow bowl.

Dredge the roasted squash rings in the dukkah, patting it in to coat evenly. Serve immediately or return the coated squash to the baking sheet and place it in the oven to reheat, about 5 minutes. Arrange the rings on a serving platter and sprinkle with fresh mint.

Any remaining dukkah will keep in an airtight container at room temperature for up to 2 weeks.

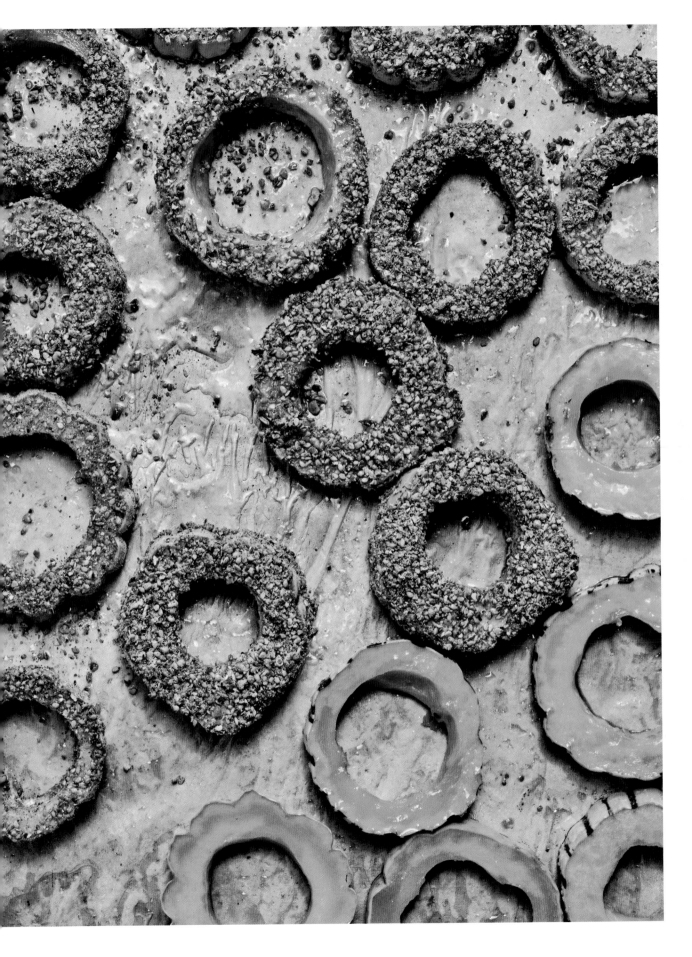

SPAGHETTI SQUASH "FIDEOS" WITH CLAMS AND CHORIZO

Makes 4 servings

Fideos is a Spanish dish of dry spaghetti sautéed in a big skillet, with shell-fish, chorizo, and white wine broth added in stages, similar to the method for making paella. Instead of using pasta, I thought it would be a fun play on the dish to use spaghetti squash, both the flesh and the seeds. The sweet strands of the squash are cooked until al dente, and the roasted seeds are blended into a rich broth that is viscous and creamy from the emulsified oils released in the process. Spiked with saffron, ginger, chiles, and smoked paprika, the resulting dish is sensual and intoxicating.

1 spaghetti squash (about 3 pounds)

2 tablespoons extra virgin olive oil

1 small yellow onion, diced

3 cloves garlic, sliced

1 fresno chile, sliced

1 bay leaf

1 sprig thyme

1 sprig marjoram or oregano, plus more chopped leaves to garnish

1 tablespoon kosher salt

1 cup dry white wine, such as Vinho Verde, Verdejo, or Albariño

1 teaspoon smoked paprika

1/2 teaspoon saffron threads

1/2 teaspoon ground cumin

1/4 teaspoon ground ginger

1/8 teaspoon ground clove

8 ounces loose chorizo sausage

One 14.5-ounce can crushed tomatoes

2 pounds littleneck clams (or at least 2 dozen)

Juice of 1 lime

Heat the oven to 375°F with racks in the upper and lower thirds.

Wash the squash well and rub the skin vigorously to remove any traces of dirt. Using a heavy knife, cut the squash in half crosswise. Use a spoon to scrape and dig out the seeds and surrounding stringy flesh into a medium bowl and save them to make the broth.

Place the halved squash cut side down in a deep roasting pan. Add a very thin layer of water to the pan, just enough to coat the bottom. Cover with a sheet of parchment paper and then a sheet of foil and cinch the foil around the edges to make a tight seal. Roast on the lower oven rack for 40 to 55 minutes. Check the doneness of the squash by pressing on it through the foil (you don't want to break the foil seal just yet). If it feels hard, continue roasting a little longer, but be careful not to overcook. When ready, it should yield just slightly to the pressure, but not feel mushy. At this point, remove the foil and flip the squash cut side up to release the steam. As soon as the squash is cool enough to handle, use a fork to separate the al dente strands from the skin. Place them in a large bowl and let cool. (The squash can be roasted up to 1 day ahead.)

Meanwhile, place the squash seeds and flesh on a rimmed baking sheet lined with parchment paper or a silicon baking mat and press them down firmly to loosen the clusters and break apart the fibers, spreading them into a single, flat layer. Bake in the upper rack of the oven above the squash halves until the seeds are toasted and the surrounding flesh is lightly browned, being careful not to let them burn, 10 to 15 minutes, stirring once halfway through.

In a medium saucepan, warm the oil over medium heat until it shimmers. Add the onions, garlic, chile, bay leaf, thyme, marjoram, and salt and cook, stirring often, until tender, about 5 minutes. Scrape the roasted squash seeds and stringy bits from the baking sheet into the pot. Add 3 cups of water, the wine, paprika, saffron, cumin, ginger, and clove and bring to a simmer. Adjust the heat to maintain a gentle simmer, partially cover, and cook for 25 minutes.

Remove the pan from the heat and discard the bay leaf and herb stems. Carefully pour the ingredients into a blender, working in batches if needed. Turn the motor on low speed and gradually increase to high, blending until smooth. Strain the broth through a fine-mesh sieve set over a large bowl and use the back of a spoon to press through as much broth as possible; discard the solids. You need about 4 cups of broth, so add more water if needed. Taste for seasoning and adjust to your liking. (The broth can be made up to 3 days ahead.)

Place a large pot with a lid over medium-high heat. Add the chorizo and cook until browned, 4 to 5 minutes. Add the tomatoes and broth and bring to a simmer. Stir in the clams, cover, and cook until the clams open, 3 to 5 minutes. Uncover and stir in the lime juice. Add the spaghetti squash and cook just to warm through. Divide the squash and clams among shallow bowls then ladle the remaining broth over the top. Garnish with lots of chopped marjoram or oregano.

SAUSAGE-STUFFED ACORN SQUASH

Makes 4 servings

I am crazy for this mash-up of sweet roasted squash stuffed with spicy sausage, crunchy pecans, and fall spices. It epitomizes the season in the most satisfying way. Acorn squash is the ideal vegetable for stuffing because of its cup-shaped form and its sturdy yet luscious texture.

2 acorn squash

¼ cup pure maple syrup

1 tablespoon plus 2 teaspoons kosher salt, plus more to taste

1 tablespoon extra virgin olive oil

3 shallots, chopped

½ cup diced red bell pepper

2 cloves garlic, minced

12 ounces ground pork, chicken, or turkey

1 teaspoon fresh thyme leaves

½ teaspoon dried sage

½ teaspoon crushed red pepper

¾ teaspoon homemade Quatre Épices (page 6), or store-bought is fine

1 cup roasted pecan pieces (see page 24)

1 tablespoon fresh lemon juice

1 tablespoon chopped flat-leaf parsley, plus more for garnish

Heat the oven to 375ºF.

Wash the squash well and rub the skin vigorously to remove any traces of dirt in the crevices. Using a heavy knife, cut each squash in half through the stem. Use a spoon to scrape and dig out the seeds and surrounding stringy flesh and save for another use.

Place the squash halves in a large roasting pan, cut sides up. Add a very thin layer of water to the pan, just enough to coat the bottom. Brush the squash flesh with the maple syrup, and season with 1 tablespoon of the salt. Cover with a sheet of parchment paper and then a sheet of foil and cinch the foil around the edges to make a tight seal. Roast until the squash is very tender when pierced with a paring knife, about 40 minutes.

Meanwhile, in a wide skillet, heat the oil over medium heat until it shimmers. Add the shallots, bell pepper, garlic, and the remaining 2 teaspoons of salt and cook until tender, about 5 minutes. Add the ground meat, thyme, sage, crushed red pepper, and quatre épices. Cook until the meat is browned and very fragrant, stirring all the while, 5 to 8 minutes. Stir in the pecans, lemon juice, and parsley. Set aside until the squash is cooked.

When ready to serve, divide the sausage mixture among the roasted squash cups and return them to the oven until warmed through, 10 to 15 minutes. Sprinkle with more parsley and serve hot.

GARAM MASALA PUMPKIN PANCAKES

Makes 12 pancakes

I have an obsession with pancakes. I love to experiment with different flours and flavor profiles, and I've found that rice flour makes a light, delicate, crispy pancake. (I prefer whole-grain brown rice flour, which can be found at natural-food stores, but white rice flour works well too.) With the addition of freshly grated raw pumpkin, and the sweet spice blend of garam masala, this pancake recipe might become your new favorite. I like the sugar pie pumpkin variety best for this recipe because of its petite size, but you can use any type of sweet squash you have on hand. Notice that the griddle is preheated before you even start mixing the batter. This ensures that the first few pancakes, which are usually toss-outs, are just as good as the last.

½ cup brown rice flour

½ cup oat flour

1 tablespoon light brown sugar

1 tablespoon Garam Masala (page 4), or store-bought is fine

1½ teaspoons baking powder

1 teaspoon baking soda

½ teaspoon kosher salt

1 large egg

1½ cups buttermilk

1 cup grated raw pumpkin

4 tablespoons unsalted butter, melted, plus more for greasing and serving

Warm honey for serving

Heat the oven to the lowest possible setting, 170° to 200°F. Heat a griddle or wide skillet over medium-high heat.

In a medium bowl, mix the brown rice flour, oat flour, brown sugar, garam masala, baking powder, baking soda, and salt. In a small bowl, lightly beat the egg and whisk in the buttermilk. Add the wet ingredients to the dry and whisk just to combine. Add the grated pumpkin and melted butter and stir to incorporate.

Check to be sure the griddle is hot by splashing it with a few drops of water; it's ready if they evaporate immediately. (If the griddle is smoking, it is too hot, so decrease the heat as needed and throughout cooking.) Grease the griddle with butter. Working in batches, drop scant ¼-cup scoops of the batter onto the griddle, being careful not to let the edges of each pancake touch. When the edges are set and bubbles form in the center, flip the pancakes and cook until golden brown on the other side, 1 to 2 minutes more. To make sure they do not get too dark, check the color by gently lifting with a spatula and taking a peek. Transfer the cooked pancakes to the warm oven to stay hot. Wipe the skillet clean and repeat to make additional pancakes, using up the remaining batter.

Stack the hot pancakes on plates and serve with softened butter and warm honey. Any leftover pancakes can be wrapped tightly and refrigerated for up to 3 days, or frozen for up to 1 month.

FISH EN PAPILLOTE WITH PATTYPAN SQUASH, FENNEL, AND LEEKS

Makes 4 servings

This classic preparation of fish, vegetables, and aromatics folded neatly into an envelope of parchment paper is a brilliant technique for a delicious impromptu meal with little effort. I like to slice the squash into thick wedges, so it doesn't cook too quickly, and layer with fennel, alliums, citrus, and a nice thick filet of white fish. Choose any mild, flaky fish, like cod, grouper, or halibut. For a fun and rustic dinner, serve the packets torn open at the table, alongside a crisp white wine, several napkins, and a good playlist.

Four 5-ounce skinless white fish filets, such as cod, grouper, or halibut

1/4 cup plus 1 tablespoon extra virgin olive oil

1 tablespoon fine sea salt

1 1/4 teaspoons freshly ground black pepper

12 ounces pattypan squash

1 fennel bulb, thinly sliced (see page 102)

1 leek, trimmed, halved, sliced, and washed well (see page 70)

4 cloves garlic, slivered

2 lemons, quartered, and seeds removed

8 fresh thyme sprigs

1 recipe Lemony Aioli (page 14)

Heat the oven to 425°F with a rack in the center. Pat the fish filets dry with paper towels and coat them on both sides with 1 tablespoon of the oil, then season them lightly with 1 teaspoon of the salt and 1/4 teaspoon of the pepper.

Place the squash on a cutting board and slice them in half through the stem end with a chef's knife. Place each half cut side down and trim away any weathered areas. Cut the squash into wedges that are about 3/4 inch wide on the skin side. To do this, angle your knife toward the center of the cut side of the squash and make radial cuts. Place the squash wedges in a bowl and set aside.

Lay out four 13-by-16-inch sheets of parchment paper. Fold the sheets in half crosswise and open them up like books. On one side, close to the crease, layer the fennel, leek, garlic, and squash, dividing them evenly. Drizzle each with about 1 tablespoon of the oil and season with 1/2 teaspoon salt and 1/4 teaspoon pepper. Place the fish on top of the vegetables. Squeeze 2 lemon wedges over each portion and add the squeezed peels to the mix. Place 2 sprigs of thyme on top of each filet.

To close each packet, fold the other half of the parchment over the ingredients. Starting at the top, begin making small, very tight overlapping folds, working your way along the outside edge of the parchment to the bottom. Twist the bottom end and fold it under the packet to seal tightly. Place the packets on a large rimmed baking sheet and bake for 12 to 15 minutes (less time for thinner filets, more for thicker filets). Let the packets rest for 5 minutes out of the oven to allow the steam to continue cooking the fish.

Place the packets on 4 large plates and tear them open at the table. Eat the fish, squash, and vegetables directly from the packets if you like, and serve the aioli on the side.

GRILLED ZUCCHINI WITH CHIMICHURRI

Makes 4 to 6 servings

Zucchini is a sponge for bold flavors. This is an exciting summer dish that shows the best this common cucurbit has to offer. You'll first salt the sliced zucchini and let it sit to draw out some of the water, which will also season the squash to the center. Chimichurri is my go-to vibrant summer sauce for all sorts of vegetables, fish, and meat. There will be plenty of extra sauce, so take advantage of the hot grill and add whatever you like to complete the meal.

4 medium zucchini

1 tablespoon kosher salt

1 tablespoon extra virgin olive oil

1 recipe Chimichurri (page 39)

Quarter the zucchini lengthwise into wedge-shaped spears (like pickle spears). Season them on all sides with the salt. Place them on a wire rack set over a large rimmed baking sheet and let sit to release some liquid, at least 20 minutes and up to 1 hour.

Heat the grill. If using gas, set to medium-high. If cooking over wood or charcoal, allow the flames to die down until the embers are glowing. If using a grill pan, place it over medium-high heat just before cooking.

Pat the zucchini dry with paper towels and brush all sides with the oil. Place the zucchini on the grill and cook on all sides (the two cut sides and the skin side) just long enough to get some good grill marks, about 3 minutes per side. Be careful not to cook the zucchini until mushy; it's best when it's still a little firm in the center.

Arrange the cooked zucchini on a platter and spoon some of the chimichurri over the top liberally. Serve the rest of the sauce on the side. This dish is delicious served warm or at room temperature.

GINGER-PECAN ZUCCHINI CRISP

Makes 6 to 8 servings

Using summer squash in baking should go far beyond zucchini bread. I wanted to experiment with treating zucchini as the fruit that it is, so I took the classic apple crisp as my cue. Afterall, when cooked until tender, there's little difference in texture between the two. Because zucchini has so much water and so little acid, I first macerate it to extract the excess juices and then simmer them into a flavorful syrup. Ginger is the power play in this surprising dessert, and pecans increase the crunch factor of the streusel topping.

3 pounds zucchini

½ cup granulated sugar

2 teaspoons apple cider vinegar

2 teaspoons fresh lemon juice

1 teaspoon kosher salt

1 cup all-purpose flour

1 cup rolled oats

1 cup chopped raw pecans

½ cup firmly packed dark brown sugar

1 teaspoon ground cinnamon

½ teaspoon ground ginger

¼ teaspoon freshly ground black pepper

½ cup (1 stick) cold unsalted butter, cut into ½-inch cubes

1 tablespoon finely grated fresh ginger

Ice cream for serving

Heat the oven to 350°F with a rack in the lower third.

Peel the zucchini and cut it into 1-inch chunks. In a large bowl, toss the zucchini with the granulated sugar, vinegar, lemon juice, and ½ teaspoon of the salt. Let stand for 30 minutes.

Meanwhile, in a medium bowl, mix ¾ cup of the flour with the oats, pecans, dark brown sugar, cinnamon, ground ginger, pepper, and remaining ½ teaspoon of salt. Using your fingers, rub the butter into the oat mixture to form pea-size clumps. Refrigerate until firm, about 10 minutes.

Transfer the zucchini mixture to a mesh strainer set over a medium saucepan. Press firmly on the squash to release as much liquid as possible. Return the squash to the bowl and set aside. Bring the strained liquid to a lively simmer over medium heat. Cook until it is reduced by about half, 5 to 6 minutes.

Stir the syrup and fresh ginger into the zucchini. Add the remaining ¼ cup flour and toss well to coat. Transfer the zucchini mixture to a 2-quart baking dish, scraping the bottom of the bowl, and spread it in an even layer. Disperse the oat mixture over the top in clumpy bits. Bake until the topping is golden brown and the filling is bubbly, 45 to 55 minutes. Serve warm, topped with ice cream.

GRILLED MARINATED CUCUMBERS

Makes 4 to 6 servings

Most people don't think about cooking the notoriously cool cucumber, but grilling brings out the sweet, juicy flavor in a new savory way. This cucumber side dish will intrigue everyone at your next cookout. If I can find them, I like to use the suyo variety, but any thin-skinned cucumber will work just fine on the grill. There will be extra marinade after the cucumbers are served, which you could reserve to toss with cold noodles or for marinating fish.

1½ pounds cucumbers, such as suyo, kirby, Persian, or English

2 tablespoons minced shallots

2 tablespoons unseasoned rice vinegar

2 tablespoons soy sauce

1 tablespoon honey

½ teaspoon crushed red pepper

1 tablespoon canola oil

3 tablespoons sliced basil or mint leaves, or a combination

1 tablespoon toasted sesame seeds

Heat the grill. If using gas, set to medium-high. If cooking over wood or charcoal, allow the flames to die down until the embers are glowing. If using a grill pan, place it over medium-high heat just before cooking.

Cut the cucumbers lengthwise in half. In a shallow baking dish, combine the shallots, vinegar, soy sauce, honey, and crushed red pepper. Add the cucumbers and turn them to coat. Place them cut side down and set aside for 10 to 15 minutes to marinate.

Remove the cucumbers from the marinade, letting excess liquid drip back into the dish, and transfer them to a rimmed baking sheet, reserving the marinade. Coat the cucumbers with the oil and place them on the grill. Cook on both sides until lightly charred and tender, 3 to 5 minutes per side.

Cut the grilled cucumbers into bite-size chunks and add them back to the reserved marinade. Toss to coat and set aside for 10 to 20 minutes before serving.

Pile the cucumbers on a serving platter or into a large bowl, and top with the herbs and sesame seeds.

SPICY SMASHED CUCUMBER AND PEACH SALAD

Makes 6 to 8 servings

The Chinese technique of smashing cucumbers provides a unique situation. Where a cucumber that has been cleanly sliced has slick edges that repel a dressing, these mangled pieces are much more receptive to a quick marinade. By tossing them in a mixture of salt and sugar, more water is extracted and the cucumber flavor becomes more concentrated. Try this alongside coconut sticky rice or as a side dish to grilled pork ribs on a hot summer day.

1½ pounds thin-skinned cucumbers, such as English, kirby, or Persian

1 teaspoon kosher salt

2 teaspoons light brown sugar

2 tablespoons fresh lime juice, plus more to taste

2 tablespoons unseasoned rice vinegar

1 tablespoon fish sauce, plus more to taste

1 tablespoon Green Chile Sambal (page 32), or store-bought sambal, plus more as needed

2 teaspoons toasted sesame oil

2 cloves garlic, minced

3 large firm-ripe peaches (about 1½ pounds)

Torn basil leaves for garnish

Place the cucumbers on a cutting board. With a rolling pin, mallet, or large, wide knife, smash each whole cucumber until the skin is split and the cucumber is a bit flattened. Using a knife or your hands, cut or pull apart each piece into random shapes and sizes based on how they naturally want to break, aiming for pieces about 1½ inches long.

Place the cucumbers in a mixing bowl and toss with the salt and brown sugar. Transfer the cucumbers to a colander set in the sink and let drain for 30 minutes.

In a small bowl, whisk the lime juice, vinegar, fish sauce, sambal, sesame oil, and garlic. Place the drained cucumbers in a resealable plastic bag and mix in the dressing. Seal the bag, pressing out the air. Marinate in the refrigerator for 30 minutes.

Peel the peaches, then cut them in half and discard the pits. Cut the peaches into 1-inch chunks and add them to the bag, jumbling the ingredients together. Reseal the bag and return it to the refrigerator to chill for at least 15 minutes or up to 1 hour. Taste for seasoning and adjust to your liking, adding more lime juice, fish sauce, or sambal as needed. Pour the contents of the bag into a large bowl and serve cold, garnished with basil.

FROTHY CUCUMBER LIMEADE

Makes 6 to 8 servings

If cucumbers are left unattended in the garden they can grow longer than expected and result in thicker skins or pithy seeds. If this happens, don't fret. You can peel the skins and scrape the seeds to make this refreshing cooler, or just grate some whole cucumber and start from scratch. I like to serve it unstrained because the cucumber adds body to this fun beverage. For an adult version, spike it with gin, vodka, or mezcal.

1 cup cucumber seeds and attached flesh, or grated whole cucumber

1 1/2 cups fresh lime juice

1 teaspoon fine sea salt

1/2 cup agave syrup

1 large handful fresh tender herb leaves, such as basil, tarragon, or mint, plus more whole sprigs for garnish

Place the cucumber, lime juice, salt, agave, and herbs in a blender. Add 1 cup of ice and 1 cup of water and blend on high speed until completely smooth and frothy, about 1 minute. Pour the limeade into glasses filled with ice. Place an herb sprig in each glass to garnish.

HONEYDEW AQUAVIT SLUSHIES

Makes 6 to 8 cocktails

While you'll feel like you're on vacation sipping it, this is not your typical frozen drink! It has a more sophisticated profile than the average adult slushie, with the savory notes of dill, salt, and aquavit against the sweetness of honeydew melon. Be sure to freeze the cut melon chunks ahead of time since they act as the ice cubes. If you've not tried aquavit before, it is essentially Scandinavia's version of gin, with caraway as the prominent flavor, and many other complexities from spices such as cumin, anise, and dill.

1 ripe honeydew melon

1½ cups aquavit

¾ cup fresh lemon juice

2 tablespoon chopped fresh dill, plus more for garnish

1 teaspoon fine sea salt

½ teaspoon freshly ground black pepper

Crushed caraway seeds for garnish

Place the melon on a large cutting board and cut it in half lengthwise. Scoop out and discard the seeds, then cut each melon half into 4 wedges. With the skin side down, run the tip of a chef's knife between the flesh and the skin to remove the peel from each wedge.

Cut the melon wedges into cubes and measure 4 cups; reserve any extra for another use (or eat it fresh!). Place the 4 cups of cubed melon in a resealable freezer bag. Lay the bag flat in the freezer with the pieces in a single layer to prevent the fruit from freezing in a clump. Freeze for at least 4 hours, but preferably overnight.

Place the frozen melon in a blender and add 2 cups of ice. Add the aquavit, lemon juice, dill, salt, and pepper. Blend on high speed until smooth, about 1 minute. Divide the slushie between glasses and garnish with crushed caraway seeds and more chopped dill.

MELON AND SHRIMP SALAD WITH CHILE VINAIGRETTE

Makes 4 servings

The first time I served this salad, I was catering an important luncheon for a close friend. The invitees were discussing funding for some school gardens, and I was hoping that they would strike a deal, so I offered to help with my services. I'd like to think that this refreshing salad helped inspire the donation. Now those school gardens are thriving.

1 ripe cantaloupe or honeydew melon

1 tablespoon extra virgin olive oil

1 pound large shrimp, peeled, deveined, and patted dry

2 cloves garlic, minced

1 teaspoon sweet paprika

1 teaspoon fine sea salt

1 recipe Chile Vinaigrette (page 19)

5 ounces baby salad greens, such as little gems, Bibb, or salanova lettuces

1 large handful fresh basil or mint leaves, or a combination

Place the melon on a large cutting board and cut it in half lengthwise. Scoop out and discard the seeds, then cut each melon half into 4 wedges. With the skin side down, run the tip of a chef's knife between the flesh and the skin to remove the peel from each wedge. Reserve half of the melon for another use. Cut the other half into wedges that are about 2 inches long and ½ inch thick. Refrigerate the melon, covered, until well chilled.

In a wide skillet, warm the oil over medium heat until it shimmers. Add the shrimp, garlic, paprika, and salt and stir to coat the shrimp in the seasonings. Cook until the shrimp turn pink and begin to curl, 3 to 4 minutes. Transfer the shrimp to a plate to cool. Immediately add the vinaigrette to the hot pan and stir, scraping up the bits from the bottom. Pour the vinaigrette back into its bowl and set aside to cool to room temperature. Once cool, toss the salad greens in a bowl with a light coating of the dressing.

Divide the salad greens among 4 plates. Scatter the melon, shrimp, and herbs over the greens, and drizzle with the remaining dressing.

CANTALOUPE GAZPACHO WITH CRISPY CURED HAM AND ALMONDS

Makes 4 to 6 servings

This gazpacho is inspired by ajoblanco, the almond-based chilled soup of Spain that's traditionally garnished with grapes or melon. But I like to add cantaloupe to the blender with the other ingredients to give the soup body and a touch of sweetness. This is a great way to use a ripe, juicy cantaloupe—or even honeydew—and it's okay if the melon is bruised or a little overripe. Because this soup is so light and fresh, I find that garnishing it with crunchy almonds and salty ham really punches up the flavor and the herbs make it sing. Marcona almonds from Spain are a luxurious addition, but any good-quality almond will do the trick. Serve the crispy ham slices whole or crushed into each bowl.

1 ripe cantaloupe

¼ cup extra virgin olive oil, plus more for drizzling

1 small Vidalia or sweet yellow onion, peeled and sliced

1 teaspoon fine sea salt

¾ cup blanched slivered almonds

1 clove garlic, sliced

¼ teaspoon piment d'Espelette (see Note on page 122), plus more for garnish

2 tablespoons fresh lemon juice

1 tablespoon sherry vinegar

4 slices Crispy Cured Ham (page 25)

⅓ cup chopped Marcona almonds or roasted slivered almonds (see page 24)

Torn fresh basil or mint leaves for garnish

Halve, seed, and peel the melon following the instructions on page 268. Cut it into cubes and measure 4½ cups; reserve any extra for another use.

In a medium saucepan, warm the oil over medium heat until it shimmers. Add the onions and salt and cook until the onions just begins to soften, stirring frequently, about 3 minutes. Add the slivered almonds, garlic, and piment d'Espelette and cook, stirring often, until the onions are completely translucent and tender and the almonds are lightly browned, 6 to 8 minutes. Remove from the heat.

Transfer the hot onion mixture to a blender. Add the cubed cantaloupe, lemon juice, and vinegar. Begin blending on low speed and gradually raise the speed to high. Blend until the mixture is velvety smooth. If the finished soup is too thick, add a splash of water, or (better yet) more cantaloupe if you have extra, and blend again. Taste for seasoning and adjust to your liking.

Pour the gazpacho into a container, cover, and refrigerate until very well chilled, at least 2 hours.

To serve, pour the gazpacho into bowls. Drizzle each with a little olive oil and sprinkle with more piment d'Espelette. Top with the crispy ham, roasted almonds, and herbs.

WATERMELON WITH TAMARIND AND LABNEH

Makes 4 to 6 servings

Around the time that we added a tiny pool onto the deck of our Atlanta home, I was experimenting with different ways to serve watermelon. I had gone to the Israeli market earlier in the week and found a bunch of tasty ingredients to play around with, so I threw this one together when some friends stopped by to hang by the pool. It was so addictive that I made it every weekend for the rest of the summer. The best thing about this recipe is that it takes no time at all—just be sure to keep the watermelon ice-cold until you're ready to dress it and serve.

1 small seedless watermelon

1 cup labneh or plain Greek yogurt

¼ cup seedless tamarind paste (see Note)

1 teaspoon flaky sea salt

¼ cup Za'atar (page 7), or store-bought is fine

1 handful fresh mint leaves, torn

Place the watermelon on a large cutting board and trim each end to expose the flesh. Stand the melon on one of the cut ends to balance it. Using the tip of the knife, carve away the skin and white flesh to reveal the pink fruit underneath. Lay the watermelon on its side and slice it crosswise into 1½-inch-thick disks. Cut each disk into pie-shaped wedges. Refrigerate in a covered container until well chilled.

Spread the labneh or yogurt across a serving platter or divide it among individual plates. Place the chilled watermelon wedges on top and drizzle with the tamarind paste. Sprinkle with the sea salt, za'atar, and mint and serve cold.

NOTE: I love Neera's seedless tamarind paste for this recipe. It has a molasses-like consistency that nicely coats the watermelon. You can also use seedless tamarind pulp that comes in a compressed block, but you will need to dissolve it in hot water to achieve the desired viscosity. You can also substitute pomegranate molasses for an equally tangy effect.

WATERMELON WITH LIME MASCARPONE

Makes 6 to 8 servings

This is a tangy, sweet, and refreshing summertime dessert snack that will transform how you think of serving watermelon. Chunks of cold, juicy watermelon are dipped into lime-scented mascarpone cheese in this ridiculously easy and healthy-ish treat that is perfect for a hot sunny day. If you want to make it fancy, layer the mascarpone mixture and the watermelon in parfait glasses just before serving.

1 small seedless watermelon

8 ounces mascarpone cheese, at room temperature

2 tablespoons powdered sugar

Zest and juice of 1 lime

1/8 teaspoon fine sea salt

Flaky sea salt for garnish

Peel the watermelon and cut it into disks following the instructions on page 274 Cut the disks into 1½-inch chunks and measure 4½ cups; reserve any extra for another use. Place the watermelon pieces in a bowl, cover, and refrigerate until well chilled.

In a medium bowl, whisk the mascarpone, powdered sugar, lime zest and juice, and fine sea salt. Transfer the dip to a serving bowl and place it on a platter. Arrange the chilled watermelon pieces around the bowl and sprinkle them with flaky sea salt. Serve with cocktail forks, or just eat with your fingers.

MUSHROOMS

Although mushrooms are fungi, culinarily they are treated as vegetables. Whether cultivated or wild, mushrooms thrive on decaying plant matter and need damp, dark environs to grow.

In the wild, they have a symbiotic relationship with trees, and are foraged by expert hunters. Consider them the wild game of the vegetarian world. Their unpredictability and elusiveness make them a prized find, and the varieties available depend on the season and region. The conditions in which cultivated mushrooms are raised mimic the natural environment, making them easy to grow. Cremini, portobello, shiitake, maitake, and a slew of other Japanese varieties are all readily available year-round in the produce department.

Whether they are cultivated or wild doesn't matter when you are cooking mushrooms, because it's all about their shape and texture. Think about them as delicate, meaty, or somewhere in between. Delicate varieties include oyster mushrooms, chanterelles, black trumpet, enoki, and beech. They are all so tender, they can be torn into pieces by hand. Honor their fragility when cooking, using thoughtful techniques that keep their shape intact. Meaty types like portobellos, porcini, hen of the woods, and lobster mushrooms can be grilled or seared like steaks. In-betweeners include shiitake, cremini, and morel. They have the versatility to work interchangeably in almost any mushroom recipe.

A note on cleaning mushrooms: Never submerge them in water unless they are covered in mud. Their porous flesh soaks up water like a sponge. Instead, use a damp brush to wipe away any dirt and debris on the surface. You can buy a special mushroom-cleaning brush, but I just use a soft-bristled paint brush.

SAUTÉED WILD MUSHROOMS AND MELTY RACLETTE CROSTINI

Makes about 20 crostini

Raclette is a washed-rind cheese that has kind of a mushroomy funk to it, and I think that's why it works so well as a blanket for mushroom-topped crostini. Chanterelle, morel, porcini, and black trumpet varieties are all nice here, but any wild mushrooms will do. These are a go-to autumn hors d'oeuvre or a luxurious lunch alongside a green salad.

1 baguette

¼ cup extra virgin olive oil

One (8-ounce) wedge raclette cheese, cold

2 tablespoon unsalted butter

1 pound wild mushrooms, such as chanterelles, morels, porcini, black trumpet, or a mix, cleaned (see page 281) and torn or cut into bite-size pieces

1 teaspoon kosher salt

1 shallot, minced

2 cloves garlic, minced

2 tablespoons finely chopped fresh parsley

1 tablespoon finely sliced fresh chive

1 tablespoon fresh lemon juice

Freshly ground black pepper

Heat the oven to 375ºF. Cut the baguette on a bias into ½-inch-thick slices (you should get about 20) and spread them out on a large rimmed baking sheet. Brush the cut sides of the slices with 2 tablespoons of the oil. Toast in the oven until golden brown on the first side, about 5 minutes. Flip them over and toast until golden brown on the second side, about 5 minutes more.

Meanwhile, trim the rind from the cheese and cut it into thin slices that are about the same size as the crostini. (It's easiest to do this when the cheese is still cold, right out of the fridge.)

In a 12-inch skillet, heat the remaining 2 tablespoons of oil and the butter over medium heat until the butter is foamy. Add the mushrooms and season with the salt. Cook, stirring occasionally, until they release their moisture and it evaporates, then let them continue to cook, stirring rarely, until they are nicely browned, 8 to 12 minutes, depending on the moisture content of the varieties you are using. Add the shallots and garlic and cook until they just begin to brown, 2 to 3 minutes. Remove the pan from the heat and stir in 1 tablespoon of the parsley, the chives, and the lemon juice. Taste a mushroom and adjust the seasoning as needed.

Heat the broiler with a rack positioned 4 to 6 inches below the heating element. Top each crostini with a spoonful of the sautéed mushrooms and then a slice of raclette, dividing them evenly. Broil for 2 to 4 minutes to just melt the cheese. Sprinkle the crostini with the remaining 1 tablespoon of parsley and a few grinds of fresh pepper, and serve them while the cheese is hot and melty.

WILD SPRING MUSHROOMS WITH ASPARAGUS

Makes 4 servings

At the peak of spring, this one-pan dish celebrates the delicacies of the season. It's a quick side dish to put together for how special it feels. The Marsala wine sauce built into the dish works especially well with roasted chicken. For a vegetarian option, spoon it over a bowl of farro or your favorite grain. I also love it with delicate steamed white fish like cod or halibut. Any mushroom varieties you see available when asparagus is in season will partner well.

1 pound wild spring mushrooms, such as chanterelle, oyster, porcini, morel, or a mix, cleaned (see page 281)

2 tablespoons extra virgin olive oil, plus more as needed

1 1/2 teaspoons kosher salt

1 pound asparagus, bottoms trimmed, cut into 2-inch pieces on a bias

2 shallots, sliced into thin rings

1 cup Marsala wine

2 tablespoon unsalted butter

If the mushrooms are quite large, cut or tear them into bite-size pieces; otherwise, leave them whole.

In a 12-inch skillet, heat the oil over medium heat until it shimmers. Add the mushrooms and season with the salt. Cook, stirring occasionally, until they release their moisture and it evaporates, then let them continue to cook, stirring rarely, until they just begin to brown, 3 to 6 minutes, depending on the moisture content of the varieties you are using. If the pan seems dry, add a little more oil, then add the asparagus and shallots and cook, stirring often, until the asparagus is tender and the shallots are wilted, 5 to 7 minutes. Tip the contents of the pan onto a serving platter and set aside briefly while you make the pan sauce.

Add the Marsala and butter to the pan and place it over medium-high heat, whisking and scraping up the bits from the bottom. Continue whisking as you cook the sauce until it is thickened enough to coat the back of a spoon. Drizzle the sauce over the mushrooms and asparagus on the platter.

MAXIMO MUSHROOM RISOTTO

Makes 4 to 6 servings

You'll find that my take on mushroom risotto is just as much about the mushrooms as the rice. In fact, the ratio is about one-to-one in the finished dish. It's really a trifecta of mushroom flavor and texture, starting with an earthy broth made with dried porcini, and utilizing both the rehydrated mushrooms from the broth and a mix of fresh varieties stirred in. Use whatever cultivated or wild varieties you find at the market and note that a combination of delicate and firm mushrooms play counterpoint to each other and the creaminess of the rice.

2 cups warm Porcini Mushroom Broth, plus the reserved strained solids (page 10)

2 tablespoons unsalted butter

1 cup carnaroli or arborio rice

1 cup dry white wine

1 tablespoon kosher salt

12 ounces mixed mushrooms, cleaned (see page 281), sliced, chopped, or hand-torn

1/2 cup heavy cream

1/2 cup freshly grated Parmigiano-Reggiano cheese, plus more for garnish

1/4 cup chopped flat-leaf parsley

After making the mushroom broth, pick out and discard the onions and thyme sprigs from the strained solids, and separate the rehydrated porcini mushrooms and garlic cloves. Chop the mushrooms and smash the garlic cloves into a paste using the edge of a knife and set aside.

Melt the butter in a 4-quart saucepan over medium heat. When the butter begins to foam, add the rice. Using a wooden spoon, cook, stirring constantly, until the rice begins to turn slightly opaque, 2 to 3 minutes. Add the wine and continue to stir until it's mostly absorbed into the rice, 3 to 4 minutes. Add one cup of the broth and 1½ teaspoons of the salt and keep stirring, leisurely rather than aggressively, until it's mostly absorbed into the rice. Add the second cup of broth along with the chopped raw mushrooms and the remaining 1½ teaspoons of salt. As you continue to stir, the mushrooms will cook down in the hot liquid and the rice will soak up the juices they release plus the broth. Once the liquid has been mostly absorbed, add the cream, the chopped porcini, and the garlic paste. Continue to cook and stir until the rice is tender but still holds a bite. This process will take a total of 25 to 30 minutes.

The finished risotto should have a creamy consistency as a whole, but the rice will have a discernible texture, and the mixture should be a little bit loose and saucy. If the rice needs to cook longer, add a touch more broth or a splash of water and stir over the heat until it's just done. Remove the pan from the heat and stir in the cheese. Taste for seasoning and adjust to your liking. Portion the hot risotto into warm bowls and garnish with more freshly grated cheese and the chopped parsley.

MUSHROOM STEM DUXELLES

Makes about 1 cup

At Miller Union, we prep a lot of mushrooms and save the stems to make duxelles, a minced mushroom condiment that's notorious as a topping for beef. I like to think of it as more than that. I see this as a vegetarian caviar and use it to elevate everything from soft-cooked eggs to grain dishes to roasted brassicas and more. You can use any part of the mushroom, but I find it to be a smart way to utilize mushroom castoffs. Use a food processor for a consistently finely minced version or chop them by hand to vary the texture depending on how you will use them.

2 tablespoons extra virgin olive oil

8 ounces mushroom stems and/or whole meaty mushrooms (oyster, porcini, king trumpet, cremini, portobello, or a mix), cleaned (see page 281) and coarsely chopped

1 teaspoon kosher salt, plus more as needed

1 shallot, finely chopped

1 clove garlic, minced

2 tablespoons dry sherry

2 tablespoons unsalted butter

2 teaspoons fresh thyme leaves

1 teaspoon balsamic vinegar

In a medium skillet, heat the olive oil over medium-high heat until it shimmers. Add the mushrooms, season with the salt, and toss to coat. Let the mushrooms cook undisturbed until lightly browned on the bottom, 3 to 4 minutes. Stir the mushrooms and continue cooking, stirring occasionally, until they are more deeply browned, about 4 minutes more. Add the shallots and garlic and cook, stirring often, until they are softened, 3 to 4 minutes. Add the sherry and scrape to deglaze the bottom of the pan, then add the butter and thyme and continue stirring until most of the liquid has evaporated. Drizzle in the vinegar, toss to coat, and remove the pan from the heat.

Taste and season with more salt, if needed. Transfer the mixture to the bowl of a food processor fitted with a blade and process until a uniform, coarse texture is achieved. Alternatively, the mushrooms can be finely minced with a chef's knife on a cutting board. Use immediately or keep the duxelles in an airtight container in the refrigerator for up to 5 days.

MISO PICKLED SHIITAKES

Makes about 1 quart

I'm obsessed with the concept of tsukemono, the Japanese method of pickling in miso. The pickling mixture is like a thick miso vinaigrette, with rice vinegar, ginger, and green onions. Shiitakes drink up the flavor like a sponge. I find the bamboo steaming technique to be a zen approach, gently cooking the mushrooms while maintaining their delicate texture and shape. They're traditionally served as an accompaniment to a meal of steamed rice and fish.

1 pound shiitake mushrooms, cleaned (see page 281)

½ cup unseasoned rice vinegar

⅓ cup white or yellow miso paste

1 bunch green onions, thinly sliced

2 cloves garlic, minced or pressed

1 tablespoon minced ginger

1 tablespoon honey

1 tablespoon tamari

1 teaspoon Korean or Thai chile powder

If the mushroom stems are tough or dried out, remove them and save them to make mushroom broth (see page 10); otherwise, leave the mushrooms whole.

If you have a two-tier bamboo steamer, divide the mushrooms between the two trays and cover with the lid. Alternatively, place the mushrooms in a steamer basket.

Fill a large pot with 1 to 2 inches of water (if you're using a bamboo steamer, a wok or pot with sloped sides works best) and set the pot over high heat until the water reaches a boil. Decrease the heat to maintain a steady simmer and carefully set the steamer over the water. Steam for 10 minutes, then turn off the heat and remove the steamer. Let the mushrooms cool to room temperature.

Combine the vinegar, miso, green onions, garlic, ginger, honey, tamari, and chile powder in a large bowl. Mix well to combine, then add the mushrooms and toss to thoroughly coat. Let sit at room temperature for 2 hours to pickle. The pickled mushrooms can be served immediately or transferred to an airtight container and refrigerated for up to 3 months.

ROASTED OYSTER MUSHROOM SALAD

Makes 4 to 6 servings

Here delicate oyster mushrooms are roasted slowly to crisp the frilly edges and concentrate their earthy, umami flavor. Tossing the warm mushrooms in a bright vinaigrette allows them to absorb the flavors in a reverse marinade effect. The seasoned mushrooms are then combined with bitter greens, juicy sweet pears, and toasty hazelnuts for a robust vegetarian main-course salad.

1 pound oyster mushrooms, cleaned (see page 281)

3 tablespoons extra virgin olive oil

1 teaspoon kosher salt

1/2 teaspoon freshly ground black pepper

1/4 to 1/3 cup Coriander Vinaigrette (page 18)

12 ounces tender, frilly salad greens, such as mizuna, baby mustard greens, frisée, or a mix

1 ripe red Bartlett or Anjou pear, quartered, cored, and thinly sliced

1/2 cup chopped roasted hazelnuts (see page 24)

Heat the oven to 375°F with a rack in the middle. Trim any tough parts at the base of each mushroom cluster and reserve to make mushroom broth (see page 10). Pull apart the clusters into individual mushrooms or smaller clusters and place them in a bowl. Add the oil, salt, and pepper and toss until the mushrooms are evenly coated. Spread the mushrooms on a rimmed baking sheet in a single layer and roast until they start to brown, 12 to 15 minutes. Remove the pan from the oven and use a fork or small spatula to turn each mushroom. Return the pan to the oven and cook until the mushrooms are nicely browned and have some crisp edges, 12 to 15 minutes more. Immediately scrape the hot mushrooms from the baking sheet into a large salad bowl and toss with 1/4 cup of the vinaigrette to coat. Set aside to cool.

When the mushrooms are cooled, add the greens, sliced pear, and hazelnuts and toss to lightly coat everything in the vinaigrette, adding a bit more if needed. Taste for seasoning and adjust as needed. Serve the salad on individual plates.

CHÈVRE-STUFFED MORELS

Makes 8 to 12 servings

The whimsical shape of magical morels reminds me of little gnome homes on the forest floor. Their hollow interior is ideal for filling, and herb-flecked goat cheese is a natural pairing with these springtime treasures. They are only available at fleeting moments, so when you see them, don't pass them by.

8 ounces chèvre cheese

1/4 cup thinly sliced fresh chives, plus more for garnish

1 teaspoon finely chopped fresh basil

1 clove garlic, grated or pressed

2 teaspoon kosher salt

1/2 teaspoon freshly ground black pepper

8 ounces medium to large morel mushrooms, cleaned (see page 281)

2 tablespoons extra virgin olive oil

Juice and zest of 1/2 lemon

Heat the oven to 375ºF. In a medium bowl, mash and mix together the chèvre, chives, basil, garlic, 1 teaspoon of the salt, and the pepper. Transfer the cheese mixture to a piping bag fitted with a wide tip. Alternatively, you can use a zip-top plastic bag with one of the bottom corners snipped as a makeshift piping bag.

One at a time, pipe the mixture into the hollow opening of each morel, filling them to the line where the stem meets the cap. Place them on a rimmed baking sheet. Drizzle the oil over each mushroom, and season them with the remaining 1 teaspoon of salt. Shake the baking sheet back and forth to coat the mushrooms in the oil and seasonings. Space them out evenly and roast until the mushrooms are tender and the filling is hot and oozy, 10 to 12 minutes. Halfway through, shake the baking sheet again and rotate it in the oven for even cooking.

Squeeze the lemon juice over the hot stuffed morels and sprinkle with the lemon zest and more chives, then serve.

PORTOBELLO FRENCH DIP WITH MUSHROOM AU JUS

Makes 4 servings

The portobello is the porterhouse of fungi, so why not treat it like a piece of meat? Get a skillet ripping hot and sear them, then make a pho-spiced mushroom au jus from the pan drippings. Then sandwich the mushrooms between a toasted baguette with melted Comté, fried onions, and a handful of fresh arugula for this veggie take on a meaty classic.

4 portobello mushrooms, cleaned (see page 281)

2 tablespoons extra virgin olive oil

1 small red onion, halved and sliced into thin, crescent-shaped wedges

1½ teaspoons kosher salt

¾ teaspoon freshly ground black pepper

3 tablespoons clarified butter or ghee

2 cups Porcini Mushroom Broth (page 10), or store-bought mushroom broth

2 cloves garlic, sliced

2 teaspoons Worcestershire sauce

1 teaspoon fresh lemon juice

10 black peppercorns

1 star anise

1 whole clove

1 baguette

One (5-ounce) block Comté cheese, cold

¼ cup Homemade Mayonnaise (page 14), or store-bought is fine

4 large handfuls arugula

Pop the stems from the portobello caps and reserve them for another use. With a small spoon, scrape away the dark gray gills from the underside of each cap and brush away any debris. Set the cleaned mushrooms aside.

Heat 1 tablespoon of the oil in a 12-inch skillet over medium heat until it shimmers. Add the onions, and season with ½ teaspoon each of the salt and pepper. Cook, stirring occasionally, until the onions are tender and lightly browned, 5 to 6 minutes. Transfer the cooked onions to a plate and set aside.

Return the skillet to the medium-high heat, and immediately add the remaining 1 tablespoon of oil and the butter. When the butter is melted, place the mushroom caps in the pan (they will be a snug fit at first, but will cook down) and sear on one side for 3 to 4 minutes. Turn the mushrooms over and sear on the other side, 3 to 4 minutes more. Add about ½ cup of the mushroom broth to the pan, and season with the remaining 1 teaspoon of salt and ¼ teaspoon of pepper. Finish cooking the mushrooms in the simmering liquid, which will deglaze the pan and tenderize the mushrooms, 3 to 5 minutes. If the mushrooms still feel a little firm but the liquid is evaporating, you can add a bit more of the broth at this point. When the mushrooms are done, transfer them to a cutting board.

Add the remaining porcini broth, the garlic, Worcestershire, lemon juice, peppercorns, star anise, and clove to the pan and bring to a simmer. Decrease the heat to low to steep while you assemble the sandwiches.

Set a rack in the center of the oven and heat the broiler to high. Cut the baguette into quarters crosswise then cut each piece in half lengthwise. Trim the rind from the cheese and cut it into thin slices. (It's easiest to do this when the cheese is still cold, right out of the fridge.)

Place the baguette pieces cut side up on a baking sheet. Layer the cheese on the cut sides of each baguette top and spread the bottoms with the mayo. Place the baking sheet under the broiler until the cheese is melted and bubbly and the bread is lightly toasted.

Cut the portobello caps in half and shingle them across the mayo side of the bread. Layer with the cooked onions and arugula, then place the tops on each sandwich, melty cheese side down. Strain the au jus through a fine-mesh sieve and divide it between 4 ramekins to serve alongside each sandwich.

MUSHROOM PÂTÉ WITH CRUDITÉS

Makes 1 pint

Long before I was a chef, I used to make a rich baked mushroom pâté that was bound with eggs, cream, and bread crumbs. Though I liked the idea then, in hindsight it was a little dense, heavy, and time-consuming. For this lightened-up version, the mushrooms are simply sautéed and blended with roasted walnuts and fresh aromatics to create a spreadable pâté that's an ideal dip to keep in the fridge for snacking. Serve it with cut radishes, celery, fennel, carrots, Belgian endive leaves, or any crisp seasonal vegetables.

2 tablespoons extra virgin olive oil, plus more as needed

1 small leek, trimmed, sliced, and washed well (see page 70)

2 cloves garlic, chopped

1½ teaspoons kosher salt

8 ounces cremini mushrooms, cleaned (see page 281), halved, and sliced

2 teaspoons fresh thyme leaves

½ cup sliced green onions, plus a little extra for garnish

1 cup roasted walnuts (see page 24)

¼ cup dry white wine

½ teaspoon freshly ground black pepper

Pinch ground nutmeg

Pinch ground clove

1 tablespoon fresh lemon juice

Fresh-cut vegetables for serving

In a large skillet, heat 1 tablespoon of the oil over medium heat until it shimmers. Add the leek, garlic, and ½ teaspoon of the salt and cook, stirring often, until tender but not brown, 3 to 4 minutes. Add the remaining 1 tablespoon of oil, the mushrooms, and ½ teaspoon of the salt and cook, stirring often, until the moisture from the mushrooms has been released and evaporated and they begin to brown, about 5 minutes. Stir in the thyme, green onions, walnuts, and remaining ½ teaspoon of salt and cook 1 to 2 minutes. Add the white wine and scrape up the bits from the bottom of the pan. (Add a splash of water if you need more liquid to further deglaze the pan.) Decrease the heat to low, cover, and cook until the walnuts have softened a bit, about 2 minutes. Stir in the pepper, nutmeg, and clove and remove the pan from the heat.

Transfer the contents of the pan to a food processor and add the lemon juice. Puree until a relatively smooth pâté forms. Taste for seasoning and adjust as needed. Spoon the pâté into a shallow bowl, drizzle with a little olive oil, and sprinkle with green onions. Serve with fresh vegetables on the side to dip or smear it on.

GRILLED MAITAKE STEAKS WITH MAÎTRE D' BUTTER

Makes 4 to 6 servings

When produce is in abundance and the grill is fired up, I could happily grill off several types of vegetables and make it a plant-forward feast. The center of the meal is often grilled maitakes with a flavored butter slowly melting into the hot mushrooms. Be sure to set the table with steak knives for this one and pull out that special bottle of red wine.

12 ounces maitake mushrooms, cleaned (see page 281)

2 tablespoons extra virgin olive oil

1 teaspoon kosher salt

½ teaspoon freshly ground black pepper

2 teaspoons fresh lemon juice

¼ cup Maître D' Butter (page 35), at room temperature

Heat the grill. If using gas, set to high. If cooking over wood or charcoal, allow the flames to die down until the embers are glowing. If using a grill pan, place it over medium-high heat just before cooking.

Trim away any tough bottom ends from the mushrooms and reserve them to make mushroom broth (see page 10). Cut each cluster in half through the base. Place them in a large bowl and toss with the oil, salt, and pepper.

Place the mushrooms cut side down on the grill, cover, and cook until they are lightly browned and grill marks appear, 3 to 4 minutes. Give them a quarter turn and continue cooking on the cut sides until they are nicely charred and have good grill marks, 3 to 4 minutes more. Flip them over and continue grilling to lightly char the edges, 4 to 5 minutes more. Remove the mushrooms from the grill and place them back in the bowl they were seasoned in. Toss them with the lemon juice.

Arrange the hot mushrooms on a platter and top with pats of the butter. If the mushrooms have cooled too much to melt the butter, simply place the platter in the oven under the broiler briefly, just before serving.

GINGERY PORK AND MUSHROOM MEAT LOAF WITH APRICOT GLAZE

Makes 6 servings

I drooled over a dish at Mister Jiu's in San Francisco on a brief visit to the city. It was a complex pork preparation with five spice and stone fruit that seduced me with this intoxicating combination. Back home, I adapted a simpler version that mixes the plant power of mushrooms with ground pork into an aromatic meat loaf slathered with sweet-and-sour dried apricot glaze.

GLAZE

2/3 cup dried apricots, chopped

1 shallot, chopped

1 tablespoon minced ginger

1 tablespoons ume vinegar or unseasoned rice vinegar

1 tablespoon honey

1/2 teaspoon five-spice powder

1 teaspoon kosher salt

MEAT LOAF

8 ounces shiitake mushrooms, cleaned (see page 281) and stems removed

8 ounces cremini mushrooms, cleaned (see page 281) and coarsely chopped

1 tablespoon peanut or vegetable oil

1 tablespoon toasted sesame oil

1 shallot, minced

1 tablespoon minced ginger

2 cloves garlic, minced

1 tablespoon kosher salt

1 pound ground pork

1 egg, beaten

3 tablespoons white or brown rice flour

1 tablespoon five-spice powder

1 tablespoon soy sauce or tamari

TO MAKE THE GLAZE: Place the dried apricots, shallots, ginger, vinegar, honey, five spice, and salt in a small saucepan and add 3/4 cup water. Bring to a lively simmer over medium heat. Remove the pan from the heat, cover, and steep until the apricots are rehydrated and plump, about 15 minutes. Transfer the ingredients to a blender and blend on high speed until smooth. Taste for seasoning and adjust to your liking, adding more honey, vinegar, or salt, as needed; it should be bold, tart, and sweet. (The sauce can be made up to three days ahead and stored in the refrigerator in an airtight container.)

TO MAKE THE MEAT LOAF: Heat the oven to 375°F with a rack in the middle. Place the shiitake caps and chopped cremini mushrooms in a food processor and blitz to a uniform, coarse texture; set aside.

In a wide skillet, heat both oils over medium heat until shimmering. Add the minced mushrooms, shallots, ginger, garlic, and salt. Cook, stirring occasionally, until the mushrooms are tender and their liquid has evaporated, 8 to 10 minutes. Remove from the heat and set aside to cool.

Combine the cooled mushroom mixture with the ground pork, egg, flour, five spice, and soy sauce in a large bowl. Mix together using your hands (I like to wear disposable gloves for this) or a rigid spoon until well combined. Transfer the mixture to a standard loaf pan and press it in an even layer. Spread 1½ cups of the apricot glaze across the top and bake, uncovered, until the temperature in the center of the meat loaf reaches 155°F on an instant-read thermometer, 45 to 50 minutes. When the juices are bubbly and the meat loaf has started to pull away from the side of the pan, it's a good sign to check for doneness.

Let the meat loaf cool for 10 minutes, then slice the and serve with any extra apricot glaze on the side.

ACKNOWLEDGMENTS

SPECIAL THANKS TO THE COOKBOOK TEAM

COAUTHOR, EDITOR, AND RECIPE TESTER, Andrea Slonecker

PHOTOGRAPHER, Andrew Thomas Lee

CULINARY ASSISTANT AND COEDITOR, Alexandra Lampert

PROP STYLIST AND ART DIRECTION, Thomas Driver

BIG THANKS TO

all of our local Atlanta-area farmers and their
beautiful seasonal produce

Judy Lampert, who provided her charming lake home
to finish our manuscript

Amy Hughes, literary agent, Amy Hughes Agency

Karen Rinaldi, publisher and editor, HarperWave

Kirby Sandmeyer, assistant editor, HarperWave

the Harrigan family, for their unwavering support

Ben Tompkins, my patient and supportive husband

the entire Miller Union team, for always keeping the
vision alive and for inspiring me every day

INDEX

Page references in italics refer to illustrations